Better Homes and Gardens®

BATH & BEDROOM PROJECTS
YOU CAN BUILD

BETTER HOMES AND GARDENS® BOOKS

Editor in Chief: James A. Autry
Editorial Director: Neil Kuehnl
Executive Art Director: William J. Yates

Editor: Gerald M. Knox
Art Director: Ernest Shelton
Associate Art Directors: Randall Yontz,
    Neoma Alt West
Assistant Art Director: Harijs Priekulis
Copy and Production Editors:
    David Kirchner, Lamont Olson,
    David A. Walsh
Senior Graphic Designer: Faith Berven
Graphic Designers: Linda Ford,
    Richard Lewis, Sheryl Veenschoten,
    Thomas Wegner

Building and Remodeling Editor:
    Noel Seney
Building Books Editor: Larry Clayton

Bath and Bedroom Projects You Can Build

Editors: Noel Seney, Larry Clayton
Associate Editor: Linda Smith
Copy and Production Editor:
    Lamont Olson
Graphic Designer: Thomas Wegner
Contributing Writer: John Sculley
Exploded Drawings: William C. Schuster

Project Design Credits
William J. Ishmael NSID, page 4; Bryce
Cann AIA, 6; Mrs. Roy Barnes, 7; Marilyn
Worseldine, 10; Keith Gasser, 12; Douglas
Knop, 14; Suzy Taylor ASID, 15, 51;
Meredyth Moses, 16, 65; Just Plain Smith
Company, 19; Gerald Tomlin ASID, 20;
David Ashe, 25, 48, 75; John Noblitt, 26;
Gary Grosbeck, 29; Berklew Design
Associates, 30; Lenore Lucey, 32; Color
Design Art, 33; Avco Community
Developers, 34; Dr. Robert O'Neal, 36,
Edith Topal, 37; Peggy Walker, 38; Robert
Dittmer, 40, 46; Jim Peterson, 42; Stephen
Mead, 49, 58; Camille Lehman ASID and
Charles Lehman FASIC, 56; Bonnie Seney,
61; Robert Edmonds, 62; Gerald R. Cugini
Associates, Architects, 66; New
Dimensions, 69; Mary Lou Shields, 71;
Bruce Abrahamson, 72; Sam Davis, 78.

CONTENTS

STORAGE STRATEGIES

This chapter contains all the ammunition you need to fight cramped closets, overflowing bookshelves, and other overcrowding caused by lack of storage. You'll find projects for just about any bath or bedroom application, from whole-wall shelving and large room dividers to small-yet-practical storage nooks and add-on cabinets.

If one or more of the projects appeals to you but needs to be tailored to suit your layout, sit down, take out a pencil and scratch paper, and make the necessary adjustments before beginning construction. Doing your homework at this point will save you the frustration of making costly measuring and cutting errors.

Read the project directions carefully, refer to the Basics section at the back of the book if questions arise, and you're all set. Many of the projects won't take more than a day to construct.

WALL-WIDE STORAGE CENTER

Small rooms are always a challenge to organize efficiently, especially when closet space is at a premium. You can use a wall unit like this one to relieve most of the clutter. It's tall, roomy, and good looking, too.

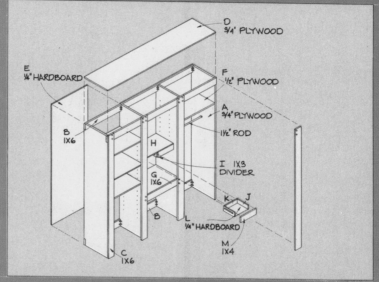

1 Cut ¾-inch plywood sides and center dividers (A). (The unit shown measures seven feet high and 18 inches deep.) Cut notches in these uprights to accept the 1×6 stretchers (B).
2 Cut the stretchers (B) to size; nail and glue them to uprights.
3 Fasten 1×6 facer boards (C) to the structure as shown with carriage bolts.
4 Cut a ¾-inch plywood top (D); glue and nail in place.
5 Nail pieces of ¼-inch hardboard (E) to the frame's back.
6 Nail a ½-inch plywood shelf (F) to the storage module at right. Attach a clothes rod.
7 Drill holes for movable shelf clips, then cut and install three more like-sized shelves (F) in the module at left.
8 Fasten the desk top (same

size as shelves) in center module with glue and nails; position it 30 inches from the floor. Nail a 1×6 support (G) beneath the desk. Secure it with carriage bolts.
9 Cut a ½-inch plywood shelf (H) for the desk. Secure it to a 1×3 divider (I). Position shelf as shown.
10 Assemble drawers as shown from 1×4 sides (J), back (K), and ¼-inch hardboard bottom (L). Rabbet the bottom into the sides and back. Nail the drawer front (M) in place. Attach drawer guides; install drawers.
11 Paint the unit as desired. Hang bamboo shades.

Materials: ¾- and ½-inch plywood, ¼-inch hardboard, 1×6, 1×4, and 1×3 lumber, clothes rod, bamboo shades, carriage bolts, nails, glue, and paint.

EASY-BUILD WALL-HUNG STORAGE

If your bathroom is short on storage space, let this wall-mounted unit help ease the crunch. The open shelving makes great display space, while doors hide less showy items such as cleansers and other bath gear.

1 Adapt this project to the space you have available. The unit shown features 1×8 shelves and measures 43×48 inches.

2 Butt together 1×8s (A, B) to form a three-sided outer frame. Assemble with nails and glue.

3 Attach 1×8 verticals (C) to the frame with nails and glue. Then, cut 1×8 shelving (D, E) to size and install between verticals.

4 Rip a 1×8 (F) to 5½ inches wide, mitering the cut at 30 degrees. Save the scrap piece (G).

5 Attach the shelf (F) between the verticals (C). Turn the scrap piece (G) to form front lip of shelf. Attach it with glue and nails.

6 Miter along both edges of a piece of ½-inch plywood (H) to form the slanted back of the rack. Glue and nail in place.

7 Attach a ½-inch plywood back (I) to the shelving unit.

8 Sink nailheads and fill with wood putty. Paint the unit.

9 Cut out ½-inch plywood doors (J, K), fill edges, and paint the doors. When dry, hinge and attach to shelf compartments as shown. Attach pulls.

10 Screw the unit to wall studs using metal angles.

Materials: ½-inch plywood, 1×8 lumber, hinges, glue, nails, wood putty, metal angles, and paint.

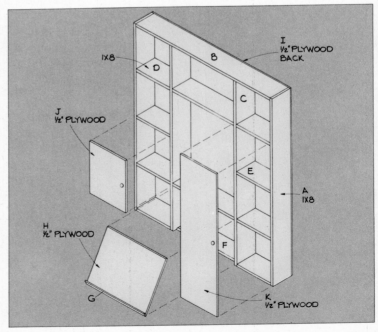

CUSTOM-BUILT LINEN CLOSET

As part of a remodeling project, this bathroom's linen closet was transformed into a tub/shower enclosure. To make up for lost space, custom-built shelves were added. Decorative molding gives the unit a professional appearance.

1 Tailor the size of the closet to your situation. The unit shown measures 43×83 inches.

2 Build two identical tall shelf modules first, using 1×8 sides (A) and top and shelves (B). Glue and nail together. Attach 1×4 facing board (C) at bottom.

3 Construct the center module from 1×8 sides (D) and shelves (E). Glue and nail together.

4 Screw the modules to each other to form a single unit.

5 Miter 1×6s (F, G) to form the boxlike top section. Add a ½-inch plywood top (H). Then nail the top section to the shelf assembly.

6 Trim the unit with molding (I, J, K, L) at top. Nail on base shoe around bottom (M, N).

7 Sink nailheads and fill with wood putty. Paint unit.

8 Cut ½-inch plywood doors (O, P, Q) to fit. Fill and sand edges and paint. Attach doors with hinges, and add magnetic catches and decorative knobs.

9 Position, then fasten the entire unit to wall studs with screws and metal angles.

Materials: ½-inch plywood, 1×8, 1×6, and 1×4 lumber, molding, hinges, catches, knobs, glue, nails, screws, metal angles, wood putty, and paint.

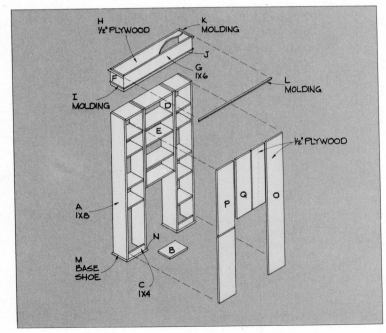

MODULAR DRESSING CENTER

Twin full-length mirrors and lots of storage make this self-contained dressing area a dream come true for any bedroom that lacks adequate closet space. The shelving offers **plenty of room for belts, purses, shoes, and other accessories. The handy pegboard back holds bulky items too large to fit on the shelves. This unit measures 48×72 inches.**

1 Working on a flat surface, cut and assemble the 1×8 frame (A, B). Secure with glue and counterbored screws.

2 Miter-cut 1×2 ledgers (C, D). These will lie flat and be flush with the back of the 1×8 frame (see sketch). Glue and nail them together.

3 Using glue and nails driven through the 1×8 frame members, join the ledgers to the frame.

4 Cut a ¼-inch perforated hardboard backing (E) to fit within the frame (A, B) and attach it to the 1×2 ledgers.

5 Rip all 1×8 divider members (F, G, H, I) to 6¼ inches wide. Cut notches in the center divider (F) to accommodate the shelf dividers (G). Using glue and counterbored screws, secure the center divider (F) to the frame.

6 Notch the shelf dividers (G), then glue and screw them in position. Do the same with members H, I.

7 Glue 1×1 trim pieces (J) to the top front edge of each shelf (see the sketch).

8 Miter 1×2s (K, L) for the two door frame assemblies. Rabbet the inside edge of each to accommodate the plywood backing (M). Glue and nail the door frames together.

9 Cut ¼-inch plywood backing sheets (M) for the doors.

10 Order two ¼-inch-thick mirror panels cut to fit within the 1×2 frame. Have handholes precut.

11 Nail the backing to the door frames, then glue the mirrors to the backing with adhesive. Cut a handhole in each plywood back.

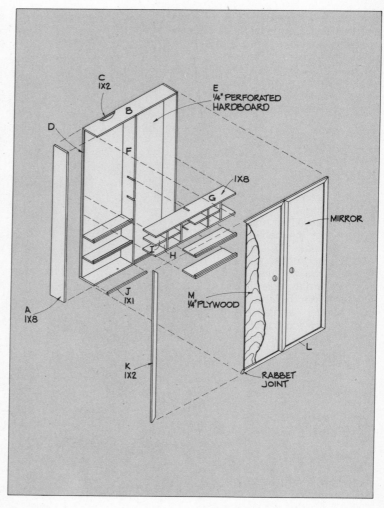

12 Sink and fill nailheads. Paint the shelf unit and the doors. After the finish is completely dry, attach the doors with long continuous hinges.

13 Hang unit by driving screws into wall studs.

Materials: ¼-inch plywood, ¼-inch perforated hardboard, 1×8, 1×2, and 1×1 lumber, ¼-inch mirror panels (with handholes precut), continuous hinges, panel adhesive, glue, nails, screws, wood putty, and paint.

BACKLIT PLANT SHELF

Build this easy overhead shelf from a couple of 2×10s, two plywood end caps, and a long fluorescent light fixture. Then, line up your favorite greenery on the shelf and see what a difference a little plant life makes in your bathroom. Your plants will love the humidity there, too.

1 Build this project to reach wall-to-wall.

2 Cut two identical lengths of 2×10 (A) for the shelf unit. Using glue and nails, fasten the shelf members together.

3 Cut the shapes shown for end caps (B) from ½-inch plywood. Glue and nail them to the shelf assembly.

4 Sink all nailheads and fill the recesses with wood putty. Paint the entire shelf unit front and back. Or, if you wish, fill and sand exposed plywood edges, stain, and apply at least two coats of polyurethane varnish. Even if you elect to stain the project, you'll still want to paint the back of vertical member A white to act as a reflective surface for the light.

5 Mount the light fixture to the shelf back. If needed, install wiring for the fixture adjacent to the shelf.

6 Install the shelf by screwing through the plywood end caps into the wall. Attach the unit to the wall studs, if possible. Otherwise, you'll need to use toggle bolts or expansion bolts to attach to the hollow wall.

7 Counterbore screwheads, fill with wood putty, and touch up with paint or stain and varnish as necessary. Complete the wiring of the light fixture.

Materials: ½-inch plywood, 2×10 lumber, one fluorescent light fixture and necessary wiring, glue, screws, toggle or expansion bolts (if necessary), nails, wood putty, and paint or stain and polyurethane varnish.

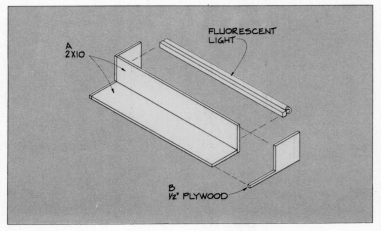

A
2X10

FLUORESCENT LIGHT

B
½" PLYWOOD

COLORFUL STORAGE HANG-UPS

If you keep a keen eye on design, even a simple storage project like the one shown here becomes an attractive bathroom treatment. Just construct a variety of colorful boxes—some with their own built-in shelving—and attach them in free-form fashion to the wall. You'll gain instant storage space plus a showcase for your special knickknacks.

1 First, decide where you want the unit. Then, on scratch paper design an attractive configuration with various sizes of boxes.
2 Cut 1×8 pieces to size for all of the boxes (A, B, C, D, E, F).
3 Assemble each box with simple butt joints. Glue and nail the members together. Add dividers as desired within the box frames.
4 Sink all nailheads and fill the recesses with wood putty. Sand smooth.
5 Paint each box assembly with at least two coats of gloss-finish paint.
6 When the paint is dry, attach one box to the next with glue and nails. Sink nailheads, fill with wood putty, and touch up with paint.
7 Locate the wall studs. Then, attach the assembly to the wall, either with small metal angles screwed to wall studs or with small ledgers screwed to the studs (use scrap 1×2 lumber).

Materials: 1×8 lumber, 1×2 ledgers *or* metal angles as needed, glue, nails, wood putty, and paint.

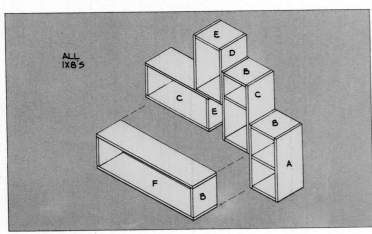

ALL 1X8'S

STYLE-RIGHT CHEST OF DRAWERS

Sleek and modern, this bedroom chest gets its stylish appearance from a carefully applied plastic laminate covering. Be sure to read the section on applying plastic laminate (see page 83) before undertaking this project.

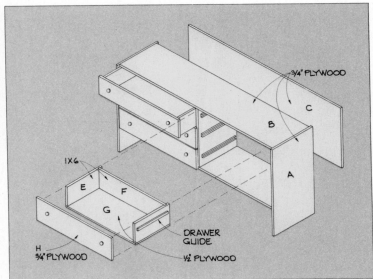

1 The outer shell of the unit shown is 30×60×16 inches.

2 Cut ¾-inch plywood sections for the sides (A), and the top and bottom (B). Glue and nail together as shown. Position the bottom so the drawers will fit flush with the top and bottom. The drawer fronts shown measure seven inches high. Allow for some space between drawers and for plastic laminate.

3 Cut the back (C) and the center divider (D) to size, then use glue and nails to attach them to A, B (see sketch).

4 Cut the drawer sides (E) and backs (F) from 1×6s. Dado the sides to accept the back (F). Also rabbet the sides and backs to accept drawer bottoms (G).

5 Cut the drawer bottoms (G) from ½-inch plywood.

6 Assemble the drawers as shown, using glue and nails.

7 Cut drawer fronts (H) from ¾-inch plywood. Nail and glue them to the drawer assemblies. Note: You must position the drawer fronts so they'll hide the divider (D) and fit flush with unit's top and bottom. Allow ⅟₁₆-inch clearance around drawers.

8 Apply adhesive and cover all exposed surfaces of the chest with plastic laminate (see instructions on page 83). Also cover the drawer fronts. Attach drawer guides, then install drawers. Drill holes; install pulls.

Materials: ¾- and ½-inch plywood, 1×6 lumber, ⅟₃₂-inch plastic laminate and adhesive, metal drawer guides, decorative pulls, glue, and nails.

EASY-REACH STORAGE CUBBYHOLES

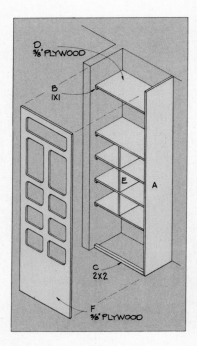

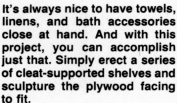

It's always nice to have towels, linens, and bath accessories close at hand. And with this project, you can accomplish just that. Simply erect a series of cleat-supported shelves and sculpture the plywood facing to fit.

1 Build the shelves floor to ceiling, making cutouts to match the height of the shelves. The project shown fits in a corner against an existing wall; if you want to position a similar unit along an open wall, build both sides from plywood.

2 For the side of the unit not adjoining the wall (A), cut a floor-to-ceiling piece of ⅜-inch plywood. Nail 1×1 ledgers (B) to the plywood at the various shelf heights. Locate the wall studs, then secure the plywood to the wall, ceiling, and floor with metal angles. Fasten a 2×2 nailer (C) to the floor.

3 Attach 1×1 shelving ledgers (B) to the wall. Cut ⅜-inch plywood shelves (D) to size. Nail the shelves to the ledgers.

4 Cut the plywood dividers (E) to size. Nail each of the dividers into position.

5 Sink nailheads and fill the recesses with wood putty. Paint the shelving as desired. Apply a primer coat first, then follow this with a coat or two of good-quality alkyd-base paint—it's specially formulated to withstand bathroom moisture.

6 Make a pattern and cut out shapes for the facing board (F) from ⅜-inch plywood. Be sure that the openings have smooth, rounded corners and are positioned to hide the center dividers and front edges of the shelving. Fill and sand exposed plywood edges. Paint to match shelving.

7 Position the facing, then nail it in place. Sink nailheads, fill the recesses with wood putty, and touch up with paint.

Materials: ⅜-inch plywood, 2×2 and 1×1 lumber, metal angles, nails, glue, wood putty, and paint.

STORES-A-LOT SHELVING DIVIDER

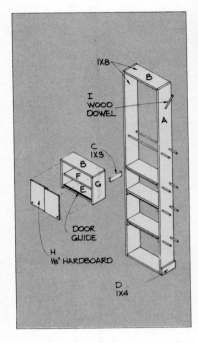

A small shelving project like this can make all the difference when bathroom storage space is limited. Every inch of it works hard—right down to the towel racks fashioned from dowels.

1 Build the unit to reach from floor to ceiling. Make the shelves as wide as space allows. The unit shown has overall measurements of 20×96×7¼ inches.

2 Cut 1×8s for the sides (A) and the top and bottom (B). Glue and nail the members together to form a boxlike frame.

3 Attach 1×3 ledgers (C) at regular intervals on the inside of the frame, gluing and nailing in place.

4 Cut additional 1×8s (same as B) for shelves; attach them to the ledgers. Also nail on 1×4 trim piece (D) at the bottom of the unit.

5 For the storage chest, dado grooves in top and bottom (B, E) for sliding doors (there are doors on both sides of the chest). Make the grooves ³⁄₁₆ inch wide and ¼ inch deep. Rip a 1×8 to 6 inches for the center shelf (F). Assemble the chest—except the top (B)—as shown.

6 Cut ⅛-inch hardboard sliding doors (H) to size. Drill holes and attach finger hole hardware. Insert doors into previously cut dadoes in the bottom (E); glue and nail on top (B).

7 Insert the chest assembly into position on the shelving unit. Glue and nail in place.

8 Drill holes for 1-inch dowel towel pegs (I). Paint the dowels, and when dry, push them into position. Use glue to secure if the fit isn't tight. Drill a hole at an angle for a single top peg.

9 Screw the shelving unit to the wall and ceiling. Counterbore screws and sink all exposed nailheads, filling with wood putty. Paint unit as desired.

Materials: ⅛-inch hardboard, 1×8, 1×4, and 1×3 lumber, finger hole hardware for doors, glue, nails, screws, wood putty, and paint.

CORNER SHELVING SYSTEM

Bright colors and interesting design come together to make this modular bathroom shelf system a joy to the eye. But visual interest isn't all this project has going for it. There's **lots of open storage space for stacking bath linens, as well as cubbyholes for showcasing curios and sculptures. Cabinets, too, add another dimension to the unit's usefulness.**

1 Plan the size and shape of various shelving units to fit whatever space is available. The following instructions apply to a unit like the one shown on the opposite page.

2 Build the L-shaped unit at the right side of the sketch first. Cut 1×8s for sides (A, B, C). Use additional lengths of 1×8 for shelves (D, E).

3 Cut two short 1×10 shelves (F) as shown. Assemble the unit by gluing and nailing the shelves between the sides (A, B, C).

4 For the top portion of the unit on the adjoining wall, first cut 1×6s (G, H, I, J, K, L) to size; rip piece L to 4¾ inches. Then using glue and nails, join the members together.

5 For the section immediately below, cut then assemble the 1×6s (M, N) using glue and nails. Glue and nail this section to the one above it.

6 For the taller of the two storage cabinets, rip 1×6s to 4¾ inches, then cut the sides (O) and the top and bottom (P) to size. Nail and glue the members together. Add 1×4 shelves (Q).

7 For the shorter cabinet, rip 1×6s to 4¾ inches, then cut the sides (R) and the top and bottom (S) to the desired size. Join the members with glue and nails. Install a 1×4 shelf (hidden in sketch).

8 Attach the cabinet units to the rest of the shelf assembly.

9 Sink all nailheads and fill the recesses with wood putty. Paint as desired.

10 Cut ¾-inch plywood doors (T, U) for the cabinets and paint.

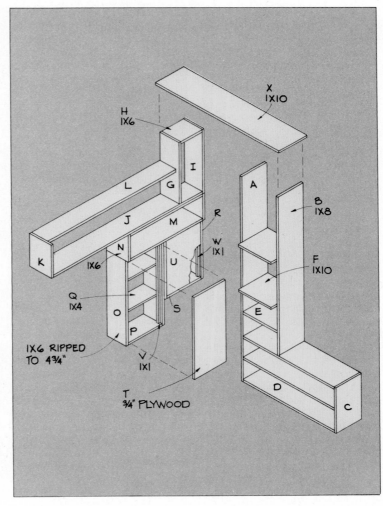

Glue 1×1 nailers (V, W) to the insides of the cabinets (see sketch). Paint the doors, then hang them using pivot hinges.

11 Attach shelving units to the wall studs using metal angles.

12 Finish the project by cutting a 1×10 top shelf (X) to size. Nail it in place and paint.

Materials: ¾-inch plywood, 1×10, 1×8, 1×6, 1×4, and 1×1 lumber, nails, wood putty, pivot hinges, metal angles, and paint.

TOWEL STORAGE CENTER

This tank-flanking shelf system gives your towels a turn for the better with its unusual vertical storage design. Extra shelves at the top and bottom offer bonus space you can always use for toiletries, plants, or decorative items.

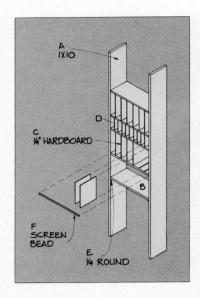

1 Cut 1×10 verticals (A) to fit from floor to ceiling. Then cut five like-size 1×10s to serve as shelves (B).

2 Cut ¼-inch-wide dadoes in the shelves (except the bottom one) to accept dividers. Allow enough space in each compartment to easily accommodate one folded towel.

3 Cut hardboard dividers (C, D) to fit. Give the shelves, dividers, and verticals two coats of alkyd-base paint. Let dry.

4 Glue and nail all the shelves except the bottom one between the uprights. Then using glue, slip the dividers into place. Let dry. Sink all nailheads, fill with wood putty, and touch up with paint as needed.

5 Cut ¼-round ledgers (E), which serve as supports for the bottom shelf. Paint before gluing and nailing to inside of uprights.

6 Trim the front of all of the shelves with screen bead molding (F) to hide the cuts you made for vertical dividers. Paint the molding before gluing it in place.

7 Use metal angles to attach the unit to the wall. Place the bottom shelf on the ledgers. Don't nail the shelf in place, because you'll want to remove it from time to time to check the tank.

Materials: ¼-inch hardboard, 1×10 lumber, ¼-round molding, screen bead molding, glue, nails, metal angles, wood putty, and paint.

STACKABLE STORAGE DRAWERS

Here's a go-anywhere system you can build to fit one storage situation and then rearrange later for another purpose. The drawer modules are portable and are stacked according to **the space available. If you want, build only the outer shell for a couple of the units and use them as cubbyholes to store items you don't mind leaving in the open.**

1 To build the outer shell for the small unit (the one shown measures 14×18×7 inches), cut the ¾-inch plywood top and bottom (A), 1×6 sides (B), and a 1×6 back (C) to size. Using glue and nails, join the members together as shown.

2 Rip 1×6s to 4⅝ inches for drawer sides (D), back (E), and front (F). Cut a ¼×¾-inch-wide dado in each side to accept the back. Glue and nail sides and back together as shown in the sketch. Cut and add the plywood bottom (G).

3 Cut a handhole in the drawer front. Glue and nail the front to the drawer assembly.

4 Cut a ¾-inch plywood top and bottom (H) for the large drawer enclosure. Also cut 1×6 sides (same size as B) and a back (I) for the unit. Glue and nail the pieces together.

5 Cut a ¾-inch plywood bottom (J) to size. Rip 1×6s for sides (same as D), back (K), and front (L) to 4⅝ inches.

6 Dado the sides (D) to accept the back. Glue and nail back, sides, and bottom together. Cut out handholes on front and complete drawer assembly.

7 Drive steel thumbtacks into the drawer bottoms to ease drawer movement. Wax the bottom to help make the drawers slide more smoothly.

8 If desired, apply two coats of polyurethane varnish.

Materials: ¾-inch plywood, 1×6 lumber, glue, nails, steel thumbtacks, wax, and polyurethane varnish (optional).

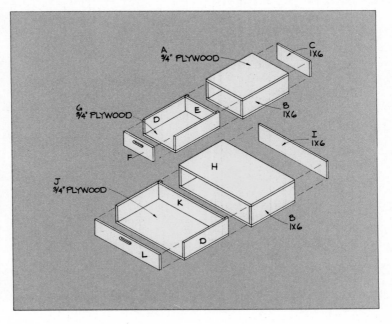

ELEGANT CLOSET ENSEMBLE

If you find yourself stealing closet space from other rooms for lack of storage space in the bedroom, then maybe you're ready for this good-looking project. The twin storage cubicles—built primarily of ¾-inch AA-grade plywood—flank a king-size bed and add more than 28 square feet of closet space.

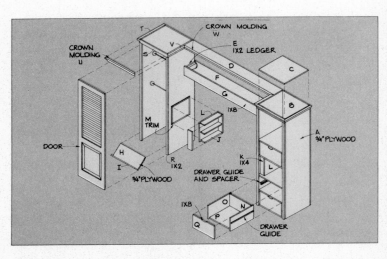

1 Build the cubicles 26 inches wide and seven feet tall. Using ¾-inch plywood, cut the sides (A) and back (B) to size. Fasten together with nails and glue.

2 Cut a top (C) for each unit. Secure in place with glue and nails. Join the two cubicles with plywood (D) fastened to the cubicles with glue and nails.

3 Install 1×2 support ledgers (E), then construct the overhead bookshelf from ¾-inch plywood (F) and a 1×8 (G).

4 In one of the cubicles, build and install a shoe rack, using plywood for both the back (H) and the lip (I). In the other cubicle, nail shelves (same as top C).

5 Cut out a section of the side of each cubicle to accommodate a square shelving niche. Assemble 1×4 shelves (J) and sides (K). Add a plywood back (L). Trim around front with mitered lattice (M). Position the niches and glue and nail them in place.

6 For the drawers, cut the 1×8 back (N), sides (O), and bottom (P) to size. Dado the sides as shown to accept the back. Notch the 1×8 drawer front (Q) for a handhold; nail to the rest of the drawer assembly.

7 Trim around front of cubicles with 1×2s (R) and 1×4 top pieces (S). Add mitered crown molding (T,U,V,W).

8 Sink and fill nailheads. Stain and varnish all surfaces. Finish two doors to match.

9 Install drawer guides. Use spacers to build out guides as necessary (see sketch).

10 Add clothes rods as shown. Hinge and attach doors. Add latch hardware and door pulls.

Materials: ¾-inch plywood, 1×8, 1×4, and 1×2 lumber, two doors and hardware, 3-inch crown molding, drawer guides, clothes rods, glue, nails, wood putty, stain, and varnish.

A BUNDLE OF BEDS

Out-of-the-ordinary bedrooms often begin with the bed itself. And though most people settle on a standard, store-bought bed to center their room around, that's not necessarily the best—or most economical—avenue to follow.

The projects in this chapter offer you another way to go. You'll find several types to choose from, including canopied classics, compact spacesavers, and a host of big, low-slung platform creations to please just about any taste.

In most cases, the bed construction is so simple you'll think there must be more to it. But there isn't. That's why it makes so much sense to build one yourself.

Flip through the next few pages. You'll probably see something that makes sense for your exact situation. And when you do, don't wait to get started. Many of the projects go together surprisingly easily.

Note: To beef up a frame for use with a waterbed, secure all joints with glue and screws and increase the number of frame supports.

EASY-BUILD TWIN BED PLATFORM

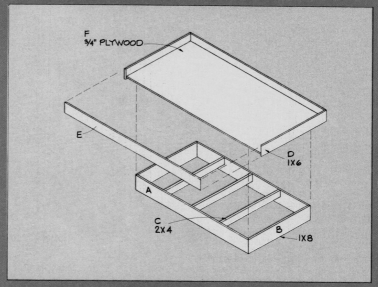

Simplicity needn't be dull, as you can see by taking a look at this no-frills project. In fact, the clean lines of the bed frame spark an interest that's often lacking in more traditional designs. Best of all, you don't need to be a woodworking wizard to get professional results.

1 A twin-size mattress measures 39×75 inches (39×80 inches for extra long). Build the mattress frame two inches wider and longer to allow room for blankets and bedspread. Build the base assembly so that the mattress frame overlaps it by three inches on both sides and five inches on both ends.

2 Miter-cut four lengths of 1×8 (A, B). Glue and nail together to form the frame for the base. Add 2×4 stretchers (C), nailing in place as shown in the sketch.

3 Miter 1×6s (D, E) for the mattress frame. Also cut platform (F) from ¾-inch plywood.

4 Nail and glue the 1×6s to the platform. Note that platform is recessed one inch within frame.

5 Glue and nail the mattress frame to base assembly.

6 Sink all nailheads; fill with wood putty. Sand all surfaces.

7 If desired, stain the wood before applying at least two coats of polyurethane varnish. Let each coat dry sufficiently and sand lightly between coats for a professional finish.

Materials: ¾-inch plywood, 2×4, 1×8, and 1×6 lumber, glue, nails, wood putty, stain (if desired), and varnish.

SPACE-SAVER FOLD-DOWN BED

Here's a modern Murphy bed with a bonus—a flip-down table that doubles as a decorative wall graphic when not in use. If you tackle this project, take extra time to figure all your dimensions and materials carefully. For easy operation of the folding bed, pay special attention to where the axle and bearings connect the bed to its enclosure.

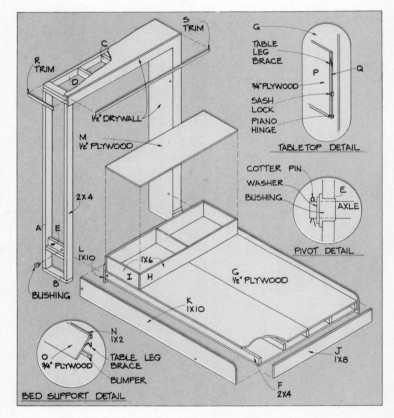

1 Build to fit the wall space available. Use a foam rubber mattress to minimize weight.

2 Construct a 2×4 frame for the bed enclosure (A, B, C, D) as shown. Anchor it to the floor, ceiling, and wall studs.

3 Calculate the location of the axle-and-bushing assembly. Install 2×4s (E) to serve as bushing supports on each side of the enclosure. Drill holes to accommodate the bushings.

4 To build the bed platform, sandwich 2×4s (F) between ½-inch plywood sheets (G). Build the ballast box (H, I) from 1×6s.

5 Skirt the frame with a 1×8 at the foot (J) and 1×10s on each side (K) and at the head (L)—see sketch. Radius the corners of the sides as shown. Fasten with glue and screws.

6 Drill holes through the bed frame (F, K) to accommodate the axle and bushings. Use scrap lumber to prop the bed platform in place within the enclosure. Line up the holes for the axle. Install bushings and axle. Check to see if bed folds up and down smoothly. If necessary, remove axle and bushings and re-drill holes in bushing supports to adjust the position of the bed.

7 Sheathe the enclosure with ½-inch drywall. Tape joints. Hide nailheads and seams with joint compound.

8 Fill the ballast box with sandbags to counterbalance the bed's weight. Nail a ½-inch plywood top (M) to the box.

9 Fold up the bed. Drill holes in each of the sides (K) and enclosure to accommodate removable ½-inch dowels.

10 Attach a 1×2 mounting board and a spacer (N) to the bed platform as shown. Mount the ¾-inch plywood bed support (O) with piano hinge. Attach locking table leg braces. Add rubber bumpers to spacer.

11 Cut a hole in the ¾-inch plywood table leg (P), then hinge it to the tabletop (Q). Use a second long hinge to attach the tabletop to the bed platform. Add locking table leg braces. Use sash locks as shown to hold the table in its closed position.

12 Nail molding (R, S) to the top of the enclosure. Paint the bed and enclosure as desired.

Materials: ¾-inch plywood, ½-inch plywood, 2×4, 1×10, 1×8, 1×6, and 1×2 lumber, ½-inch drywall, joint compound and tape, bushings and axle, piano hinges, table leg braces, glue, screws, nails, and paint.

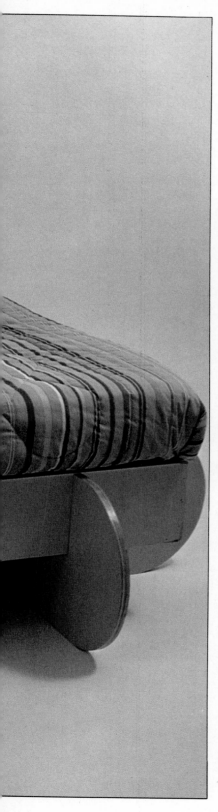

FREE-SPIRIT PLATFORM

The unusual honeycomb-style base makes this king-size platform bed the focal point of any room. A design like this demands attention, so dress it up with a stunning quilt or bedspread to show it off.

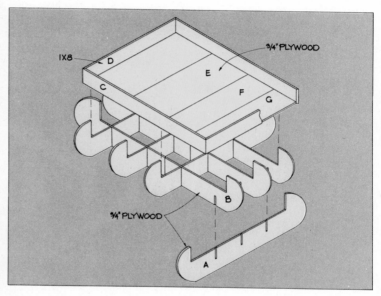

1 Although this project is designed for a king-sized bed, you can use a similar structure for a queen-size or double bed. Make the platform and frame at least two inches wider and longer than your box spring.

2 Draw a pattern for one base support to fit the width of the platform and frame (A). Cut the shape from a sheet of ¾-inch plywood. Using this piece as a guide, cut three more identical supports.

3 Following a similar procedure, cut six identical plywood shapes as shown for the lengthwise supports (B). (Note that these supports run only half the length of the platform and meet in middle.)

4 Cut ¾-inch-wide notches halfway through the supports (A, B)—see sketch. Lap the members to form a grid-like base. To ensure a tight fit, secure the members with glue.

5 Miter 1×8s (C, D) to form a frame for the box spring. Glue and nail together, then glue and nail the frame to the base supports (A, B).

6 Cut a platform from ¾-inch plywood (E). Fill out the platform area with usable plywood scraps (F, G) left over from cutting the base supports.

7 Nail the platform sections in place. Use plenty of nails to help secure the base support grid.

8 Sand and fill exposed plywood edges. Stain or paint the bed as desired.

Materials: ¾-inch plywood, 1×8 lumber, glue, finishing nails, and stain or paint.

FUTURISTIC FOUR-POSTER

This modern-style bed is simple in design and built to stay solid. It gets its strength from a sub-platform support that takes the weight off the four bedposts. That way, there's little chance for wobble or loose joints. Cover the frame with fabric to match your decorative scheme. You'll have a dramatic update of the classic four-poster.

1 Size the bed to accommodate the mattress you have.

2 For the sub-platform support, miter 1×6s (A, B), then glue and nail the members together. Strengthen the joints with scrap wood blocks; screw through the 1×6s into the blocks.

3 Separately construct a frame for the platform. Miter 1×8s (C, D), assembling with glue and nails. Attach 2×4 ledgers (E, F) along the inside bottom edge of the frame. Nail through the 1×8s into the 2×4s. Nail additional crosspieces (F) into frame.

4 Position the previously assembled sub-platform (A, B) approximately where you want to locate the bed. Rest the upper platform assembly (C, D, E, F) on the sub-platform and attach the two units with metal angles.

5 Cut ⅝-inch plywood (G) for platform sections. Nail them to frame members E and F.

6 Rabbet the tops of four 3×3s (H) as shown in the sketch to form bedposts. Position one at each corner of the platform frame; attach by screwing through piece D into posts. Use lag bolts or long wood screws dipped in glue for extra strength.

7 Cut 3×3s (I, J) for the top crosspieces. Rabbet the ends of each as shown and attach to the bedposts with screws and glue (see sketch detail).

8 Be sure the bed is positioned in room as desired. If you want, anchor the bed posts to the floor with metal angles.

9 Cover the frame and the post assemblies with your choice of fabric. Or if desired, sink nail-heads and counterbore screws, fill all recesses with wood putty (or dowel plugs for the screws), and stain and varnish the bed frame instead of covering with fabric.

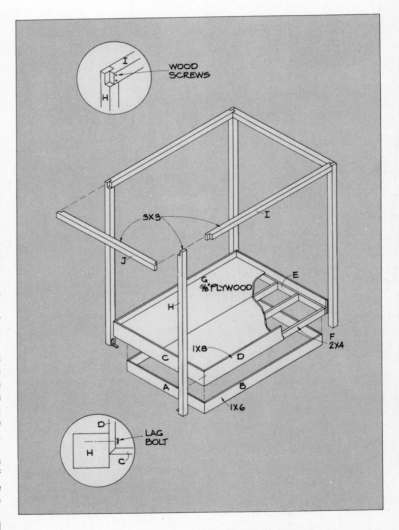

Materials: ⅝-inch interior plywood, 3×3, 2×4, 1×8, and 1×6 lumber, metal angles (optional), glue, screws, lag bolts, nails, and fabric or the stain of your choice and varnish.

KING-SIZE COMFORT ISLAND

Flanked by side tables stretching wall-to-wall, this handsome platform bed has the good looks and quality construction you look for whenever you shop for fine furniture. Build it yourself for a fraction of its showroom cost.

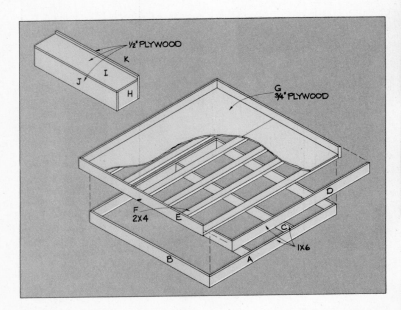

1 Build the mattress platform slightly larger than your mattress. The tables are 10½ inches tall and 12½ inches deep. Recess the platform base four inches on all sides.

2 Miter four 1×6s (A, B) for the base. Glue and nail the members together as shown. Add two 1×6 stretchers (C).

3 Cut mitered 1×6s (D, E) for the mattress frame. Glue and nail the members together. To strengthen the frame, nail 2×4 stretchers (F) flush with the bottom of the frame (D, E). Attach the entire assembly to the base unit with glue and nails.

4 Cut ¾-inch plywood sections (G) to form the platform. Nail in place.

5 Assemble the matching side tables from ½-inch plywood. Cut out the ends (H), top (I), front (J), and back (K). Glue and nail the members together as shown in the sketch using simple butt joints. Note that the back (K) extends 1½ inches above the top.

6 Sink all exposed nailheads and fill the recesses with wood putty. Glue wood veneer tape to all exposed plywood edges. Stain (if desired) and apply at least two coats of polyurethane varnish. Or, if desired, fill and sand the plywood edges and paint the unit.

Materials: ¾- and ½-inch plywood, 2×4 and 1×6 lumber, glue, nails, wood veneer tape, wood putty (optional), and stain and polyurethane varnish or good-quality paint.

BOOKCASE BED

With handy bookshelves fore and aft, this low-line platform bed is ideal for rooms large enough to accommodate a freestanding unit. It's built entirely from plywood, so it's an easy project—about a day's worth of cutting and assembling plus an extra day or two for finishing.

1 Build the platform approximately the same length and width as the mattress. And size the bookcases so that they are the same width as the mattress platform.

2 To build the bookcase assemblies, first cut out the plywood back (A), top and bottom (B), center shelf (C), and sides (D). Then glue and nail the members together as shown in the sketch, using simple butt joints.

3 For the bed platform cut the plywood base (E, F) and platform sections (G). Use additional plywood stretchers (same size as F) for extra support. Glue and screw all pieces together. Note that the platform sections (G) overhang the sides of the base (E) a few inches.

4 Screw the back of the bookcase assemblies (A) to the bed frame (F) from inside the bookcase. This allows for quick disassembly if you ever want to move the bed unit.

5 Sink all nailheads and counterbore screws (except for those attaching the bookcases to the bed). Fill the recesses with wood putty and sand.

6 Cover all of the raw plywood edges with matching wood veneer tape. Or fill edges with wood putty and sand smooth. Stain if desired. Finish all surfaces with at least two coats of polyurethane varnish.

Materials: ¾-inch plywood, wood veneer tape, wood putty (optional), glue, nails, screws, stain (if desired), and polyurethane varnish.

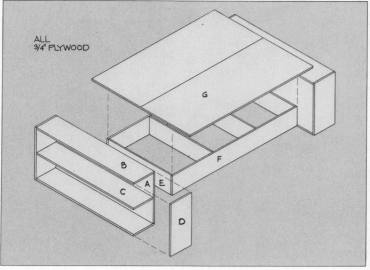

ALL ¾" PLYWOOD

CLEAN-LINED PLATFORM AND NIGHT TABLES

This sleek platform ensemble pulls together the bedroom's entire decorative scheme. If your sleeping quarters are a bit out of sync, try a similar solution substituting your colors and graphics. The mirrored bases of the bed and the night tables help to unify any room, and you can choose stunning bed linens to eliminate that dull look once and for all!

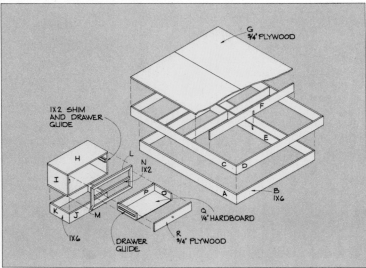

1 Build the platform to fit your mattress. The night tables are 18½ inches high.

2 Miter 1×6s (A, B) to form the base for the platform frame. Glue and nail the members together.

3 Glue and nail mitered 1×6s (C, D) together to form the platform frame. Cut ¾×2¾-inch-deep notches in the 1×6 center support (E) and secure within the frame with glue and nails. Cut a ¾×2¾-inch-deep notch in the center of the 1×6 stretchers (F). Slip stretchers into position.

4 Attach the frame to the base with metal angles. Screw platform sections (G) in place.

5 For each night table, build a frame (H, I) from ¾-inch plywood. Glue and nail together.

6 Miter 1×6s (J, K) for the table base. Nail the frame to the base. Face the exposed plywood edges at the front of the unit with 1×2s (L, M, N) as shown.

7 For the drawers, cut the sides (O) and the back (P) from ¾-inch plywood. Dado the sides to accept the back; rabbet the sides and back to accommodate the ¼-inch hardboard bottom (Q).

8 Mount drawer guides, shimming the frame with 1×2s (see sketch). Cut and attach the drawer front (R).

9 Fill and sand plywood edges. Sink and fill nailheads. Paint bed and tables; cover bases with mirror foil. Attach drawer pulls.

Materials: ¾-inch plywood, ¼-inch hardboard, 1×6 and 1×2 lumber, drawer guides and pulls, mirror foil, glue, nails, screws, wood putty, and paint.

YOUTHFUL SHIPMATE'S BUNK

Young sailors and landlubbers alike will appreciate this fanciful bedroom creation. Besides being ideal quarters for those long overnight voyages, this youth bed can double as extra seating when friends visit. You'll like the project, too. You'll have it built and outfitted before you know it.

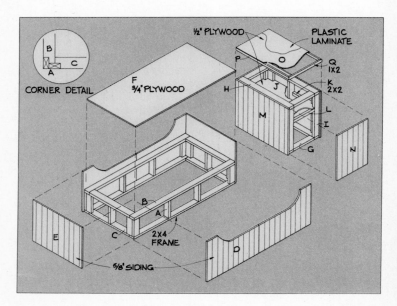

1 The bed and end table are separate units, so plan the dimensions of each to fit your needs. Make the bed at least 20 inches high; the one shown is about 24 inches high.

2 Construct a frame for the bed from 2×4s (A, B, C). Nail the members together as shown.

3 To make the bed's sculptured front panel (D), you'll need to lay two sheets of ⅝-inch-thick channel-groove siding side by side, mark the pattern, then cut the sheets individually. Then, using the front panel as a pattern, cut another panel for the opposite side. Nail both panels to the frame.

4 Cut the bed's end panels (E) from ⅝-inch siding. Again, nail to the frame.

5 Nail a ¾-inch plywood platform (F) to the 2×4 frame.

6 Build a frame for the end table from 2×4s (G, H, I). Strengthen the frame with a piece of ½-inch plywood (J), notching it to fit as needed. Support the plywood brace with 2×2 ledgers (K, L).

7 Cut the side and front and back panels (M, N) to size. Nail the panels to the frame.

8 Frame the ½-inch plywood top panel (O) with mitered 1×2s (P, Q). Glue and nail together. Attach the top to the frame. Cover the tabletop with plastic laminate (see page 83).

9 Paint the bed and end table.

Materials: ¾- and ½-inch plywood, ⅝-inch channel-groove siding, 2×4, 2×2, and 1×2 lumber, glue, nails, plastic laminate and adhesive, and paint.

ROCKABYE BABY BED

1 Cut a ¾-inch plywood bottom (A) a couple of inches longer and wider than the mattress. Frame around the underside with mitered 2×2s (B, C). Glue and nail the members together.

2 Make a frame from mitered 2×2s (same as B, C above) to serve as top rails for the crib. Cut four plywood gussets (D) for strength and glue them to the underside of the 2×2 top rails (see detail).

3 Cut two 1×2 center rails (E).

4 Line up the top frame and center rails with the bottom platform. Clamp together. Drill ½-inch holes at about 3½-inch intervals to accept dowels. Remove clamps.

5 Glue dowels (F) into crib bottom. Push center rails onto dowels, then using brads, nail in place. Glue the top 2×2 frame to the dowels.

6 To create the "gate," saw several dowels as shown, then cut out a section of the top frame (see sketch).

7 Frame the gate opening with 1×2s (G). Assemble the gate from dowels and 1×2s (H, I).

8 Fill all plywood edges with wood putty, then varnish the crib. Install the gate using butt hinges and bolt latches.

9 Attach eyebolts to the bottom frame and to the ceiling joists. Suspend the crib with rope. Tie the rope at the ceiling beneath the eyebolts.

Materials: ¾-inch plywood, 2×2 and 1×2 lumber, ½-inch dowels, rope, eyebolts, glue, nails, wood putty, and varnish.

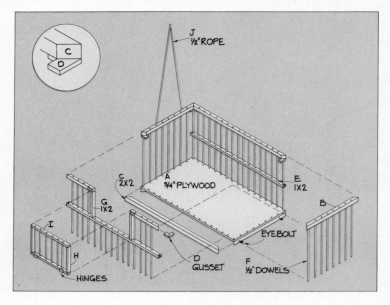

SIX-DRAWER PLATFORM BED

Kids will be forever stashing things under their bed—not much you can do about that. So why not give them lots of under-bed storage? Here's how.

1 Size the platform and frame so they are at least two inches wider and longer than the mattress. The drawer units shown measure 36×15 inches.

2 Cut the platform (A) from ¾-inch plywood. Frame around it with mitered 1×3s (B, C) as shown. Glue and nail the members together.

3 Build three identical boxlike frames for the drawer units from ½-inch plywood. Cut top and bottom (D) and sides (E), mount drawer guides, and assemble the frames with glue and nails.

4 For the drawers, cut 1×8 sides (F), back (G), bottom (H), and front (I). Make a ¾×¼-inch-deep dado in the sides to accommodate the back. Glue and nail drawers together as shown. Add drawer guides.

5 Mount a 1×2 frame (J, K) on edge to create a toespace under the drawers.

6 Space the drawer units equally and nail the platform assembly to them.

7 Sink nailheads and fill the recesses with wood putty. Paint the bed unit as desired. Install drawer pulls.

Materials: ¾- and ½-inch plywood, 1×8, 1×3, and 1×2 lumber, drawer pulls and guides, glue, finishing nails, wood putty, and paint.

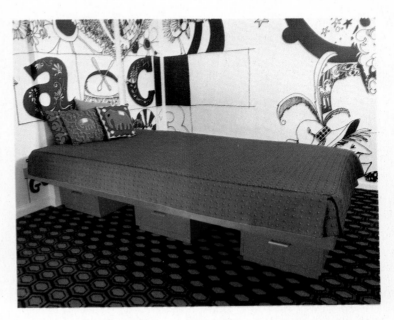

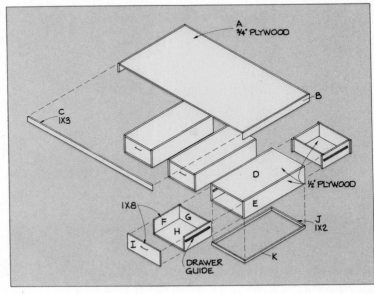

HIGH-LOW STORAGE BUNK

This colorful, bunk-like sleeper unit packs a lot of usefulness into a little space. The compartments above are designed for light storage only. You can put heavier objects below the bed platform by flipping open one of the false drawer fronts.

1 Build the bed platform and frame to fit your mattress. The unit shown is seven feet tall.

2 Begin by cutting then gluing and screwing together the ¾-inch plywood platform support members (A, B) there is only one member B. Top them with the platform (C). You'll need to notch it to accommodate the 1×3 uprights to be added later.

3 Glue and screw 1×3s (D, E) together at right angles to form the uprights. Note that member ''D'' is 2½ inches shorter than ''E'' so it will accommodate the top crosspiece.

4 Working on a flat surface, construct the sides of the bed. Tie the tops of the uprights together by gluing and screwing crosspieces (F) in place as shown. Next secure a 1×6 stretcher (G) to the inside of upright member D at upper level shelf height. Complete the front side of the bed by positioning and securing members H, I, J, and K from the backside with glue and metal straps.

5 Lift the sides of the unit into position and secure them to the platform members with glue and screws.

6 Tie the uprights together at the ends with 1×3 crosspieces (L). Toenail the members, or cut

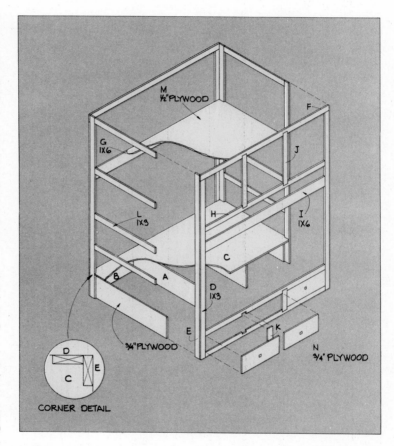

CORNER DETAIL

notches in the uprights and glue and nail.

7 Cut the ½-inch plywood shelf (M) to size (notch edges as necessary). Nail in place.

8 Fill plywood edges and other recesses with wood putty, then give all surfaces that will be exposed two coats of paint.

9 Cut the false drawer fronts (N) from ¾-inch plywood. Fill edges with wood putty, then paint. After

the paint dries, hinge the plywood at the bottom. Add drawer pulls and magnetic catches.

10 Hang window shades as shown in the photo to conceal the upper storage area.

Materials: ¾- and ½-inch plywood, 1×6 and 1×3 lumber, magnetic catches, hinges, pulls, window shades, glue, screws, nails, wood putty, and paint.

SHIPSHAPE SAILBOAT BED

Just think how your little skipper would love to captain this craft and sail it away into dreamland each night. A happy sailor he (or she) will be. It's a worthy ship rigged for snug comfort.

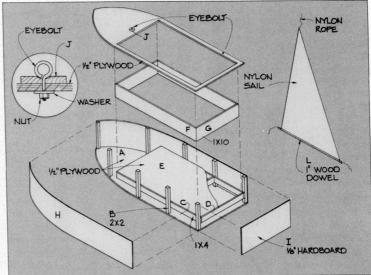

1 Build the mattress frame and platform one inch larger than the mattress. This bed is eight feet long and 18 inches tall.

2 Draw a boat-shaped pattern on a sheet of ½-inch plywood for the bottom (A). Cut out the shape and use it as a pattern for an identical plywood top.

3 Cut 2×2 verticals (B). Shape as necessary to fit contour of boat sides. Screw through the bottom (A) to attach. Counterbore screwheads.

4 Nail together the 1×4 mattress platform frame (C, D). Attach to 2×2 verticals (B) with screws. Nail the ½-inch plywood platform (E) to the frame.

5 Build the mattress frame from mitered 1×10s (F, G). Position the frame on the platform and nail it to the supports (B). The top of the frame is flush with top of the verticals.

6 Glue and nail ⅛-inch hardboard (H, I) to the sides.

7 Cut an opening in the plywood deck. Cut out a five-inch circular disc (J) from scrap plywood. Attach it to the deck with an eyebolt (see detail). Attach another eyebolt to the deck to secure the rear portion of the boom.

8 Nail the deck in place. Sink all nailheads and fill with wood putty. Paint the boat.

9 Install a one-inch diameter dowel (L) as the boom. Rig the sail from nylon cloth and rope.

Materials: ½-inch plywood, ⅛-inch hardboard, 2×2, 1×10, and 1×4 lumber, one-inch dowel, fabric and rope, glue, screws, nails, and paint.

JUST FOR KIDS

If you want to test the mettle of a piece of furniture, put it in the kids' room. If it isn't built to take lots of wear and tear (plus an occasional dose of cruel and unusual punishment) chances are it won't last long.

One good way to protect your furniture investment is to be your own skilled craftsman, and that's easier than it sounds. All you need are good ideas, some basic construction know-how, and easy-to-follow instructions.

You'll find that the projects in this chapter are just right for all kinds of room situations. Bouncy beds, lots of easy-reach storage, and decorative accents with a touch of whimsy abound. They're the kind of projects kids love—bright, colorful, yet with practicality built in.

You'll love the ideas, too. Start right away on one that catches your fancy!

STORYTIME DREAM BED

This whimsical lattice headboard has the airy appeal of a vine-covered trellis. But don't let the delicate appearance fool you. It's attached to a bed that's sturdy enough to withstand plenty of hard use.

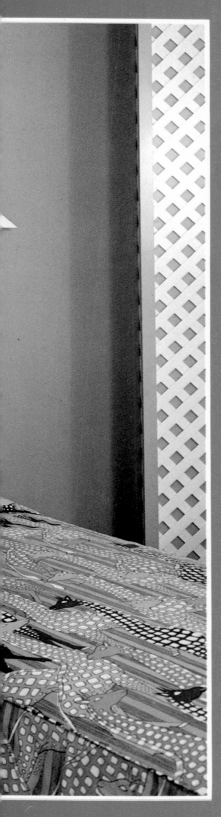

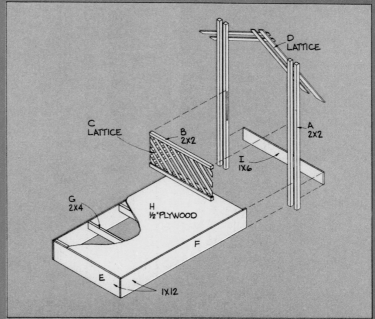

1 Tailor the bed frame and headboard to fit the mattress you have. Note that the bed frame fits between the headboard's inner pair of 2x2s. Build the headboard on a flat surface.

2 Cut four 2x2 uprights (A) for the headboard. Set two aside; cut a ½-inch groove in the other two for the lattice panel.

3 Cut 2x2s (B) for the headboard frame; groove as before to accept lattice.

4 Trim lattice strips (C) and glue them together to form a crisscross pattern. Weight down until the glue dries.

5 Lay glue in the previously cut grooves, then assemble the headboard. Secure with nails.

6 Cut and glue lattice (D) to the top of the uprights.

7 Using screws and glue, construct the bed frame from 1x12s (E,F). Add 2x4 stretchers (G).

8 Cut a ½-inch plywood platform (H). Glue and nail in place.

9 Lift the headboard into position against the bed frame and screw together. Fasten remaining two uprights (A) with screws. Screw 1x6 crossmember (I) to verticals (A).

10 Counterbore screws, sink nailheads, fill, and paint.

Materials: ½-inch plywood, 2x4, 2x2, 1x6 and 1x12 lumber, ¼-inch-thick lattice, screws, nails, glue, wood putty, and paint.

MINI-DESK FOR MINI-KIDS

When they're not scooting around the room on their easy-rolling desk chairs, your children will spend many happy hours sitting at this rugged, washable play desk.

1 Build the desk 16 inches wide. Install it at a comfortable height for the children. Let the same comfort rule apply for the chairs, too (nothing's more frustrating for kids than feet that won't reach the floor).

2 Cut the desk surface (A) from ¾-inch plywood. Frame around the sides and front with mitered 1x2s (B,C). Glue and nail the members together.

3 Cover the desk surface and the edges with plastic laminate (see instructions on page 83). Attach this part of the project to wall studs with shelf brackets.

4 Cut the sides (D) and the back (E) for each chair from ¾-inch plywood.

5 The seat and chair bottom are the same size (F). Cut both from ¾-inch plywood.

6 Glue and nail the chairs together as shown. Sink nailheads and fill with wood putty.

7 Sand all surfaces smooth and paint the chairs. You'll need two or more coats. When the paint is completely dry, install cushions and attach plate casters to the bottom of each chair.

Materials: ¾-inch plywood, 1x2 lumber, plastic laminate and adhesive, four plate casters (each chair), heavy-duty shelf brackets, nails, glue, wood putty, and your choice of paint.

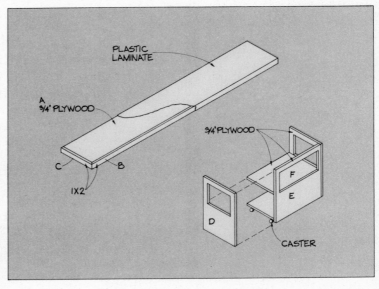

THIS 'N' THAT CATCH-ALL

Toy cleanup time isn't the most joyous part of the day for most children or their parents. But you can help. Here's a smart storage solution that even kids won't mind tossing toys and whatnot into. And it's oh-so-easy to build.

1 Purchase a ladder that's long enough to meet your storage needs. Build the support frame at least 16 inches high and wide enough to accommodate the ladder. If desired, substitute a handmade ladder for the store-bought one. Assemble it from one-inch dowels framed by good-quality 2x4s.

2 Glue and nail together the 2x2 support frame (A,B,C) as shown in the sketch. Use simple butt joints, sinking nailheads and filling the depressions with wood putty.

3 Using screws and glue, attach the ladder (D) to the inside of the frame uprights (A). Be sure that the top of the ladder is flush with the top of the uprights.

4 Sand all surfaces as necessary and apply two coats of polyurethane varnish. Or paint the unit if desired.

5 Sew together storage pouches from medium-weight canvas. Double-stitch the seams for strength. Either sew or use metal grommets to fasten the pouches together with additional strips of canvas.

6 Drape one pouch into each compartment between the ladder rungs as shown. Secure the last pouch on either end to the last rungs of the ladder by looping the canvas strip and double-stitching.

Materials: 2x2 lumber, ladder (or one-inch dowels and 2x4s), medium-weight canvas in assorted colors, heavy thread, glue, nails, screws, wood putty, and polyurethane varnish or paint.

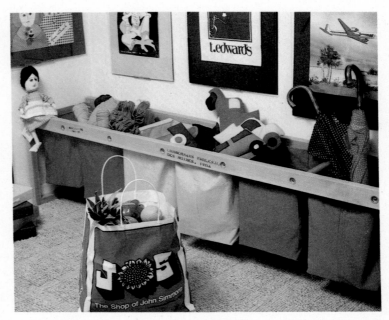

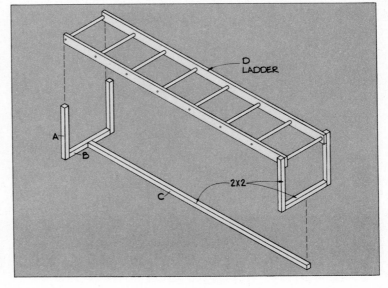

SPACE-SAVER BED/DESK ENSEMBLE

Clever design and plenty of practicality make this wall-hugging arrangement a success in any youngster's room. Note the corkboard wall next to the desk—a great way to handle those pinups and posters.

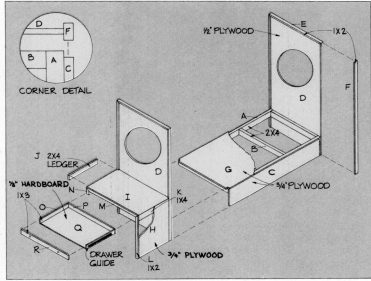

1 Build a frame for the bed platform from 2x4s (A,B). Attach a length of ¾-inch plywood (C) to form the side of the bed opposite the wall (see detail).

2 Cut a large circle from two identical ½-inch plywood panels (D). Glue and nail mitered 1x2s (E,F) around edges of panels. Nail assemblies to head and foot of bed (see detail).

3 Screw the 2x4 frame (A) to the wall studs. Cut a mattress platform (G) from ¾-inch plywood. Notch to fit around headboard and footboard. Nail in place.

4 Miter along edges of two ¾-inch plywood panels to form desk side (H) and top (I). Notch top to fit around footboard. Glue and nail together at mitered edge; strengthen the desk by nailing ledgers (J,K) as shown.

5 Position the desk, then glue and screw it to the bed. Further stabilize the desk by nailing the 2x4 ledger (J) to the wall studs. Trim around the front edge of the desk with mitered 1x2s (L,M,N).

6 Cut the sides (O) and back (P) for the desk drawer. Rabbet them to accommodate the ⅛-inch hardboard bottom (Q). Assemble the drawer. Nail the drawer front (R) to the drawer assembly and install guides.

7 Sink nailheads and fill with wood putty. Paint the unit. When the unit is completely dry, fasten pulls to the drawer front.

Materials: ¾-inch and ½-inch plywood, ⅛-inch hardboard, 2x4, 1x4, 1x3, and 1x2 lumber, drawer hardware, glue, nails, wood putty, and paint.

EVER-READY STORAGE BINS

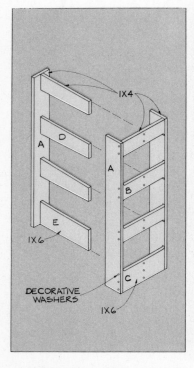

Storage space almost always is hard to come by in children's rooms. That's why this free-standing unit is so nice to have around. It's space-effective, yet accessible enough to store a surprising quantity of "very special things."

1 The wooden stand shown here is designed to hold three large kitchen wastebaskets measuring 12x9x14 inches each. You can figure your dimensions to fit whatever size containers you decide to use.

2 Cut three 1x4 verticals (A). Cut three 1x4 stretchers (B) and a 1x6 bottom stretcher (C) to fit between the two front verticals. NOTE: Radius the ends of each stretcher slightly (see sketch) to accept the wastebaskets.

3 Using glue and screws with decorative washers, fasten the stretchers to the verticals.

4 Cut basket supports from 1x4s (D) and a 1x6 bottom support (E). Taper along the length of each support as necessary to fit the shape of the baskets.

5 Glue and screw each basket support to the back vertical (A) and then to the stretchers (B,C). Again, use decorative washers for a finished look.

6 To achieve an extra rugged finish, apply at least two coats of polyurethane varnish to the stand. Or if you prefer, paint the unit. When the finish dries, insert the baskets.

7 (Optional) Cut three 1x2 "stops" to prevent an overflow of toys from tumbling out of the baskets. To hold in place, wedge a 1x2 lengthwise into the mouth of each basket.

Materials: 1x6, 1x4, and 1x2 lumber, three large plastic wastebaskets, screws, decorative washers, glue, and polyurethane varnish.

LONG 'N' LEAN DRESSING MIRROR

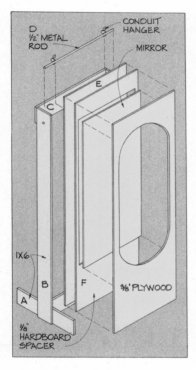

If you've been on the lookout for a good-looking yet practical accent for your child's room, this project may be just the thing. Besides being quite easy to build, it undoubtedly will be one of the most-used items in the room.

1 Construct the stand from 1x6 lumber (the stand shown is 28x72 inches). Cut three boards for the base (A); glue and nail the members together.

2 Attach 1x6 uprights (B) with glue and screws. Add a 1x6 stretcher (C) at the top to stabilize the mirror stand.

3 Drill a hole five inches from the top of each of the uprights to accommodate a ½-inch metal rod (D). To ensure a snug fit, you'll want to drill the holes slightly undersized. Insert the rod.

4 Apply two coats of polyurethane varnish to the stand.

5 Cut two 24x72-inch pieces of ⅜-inch plywood (E) to serve as the mirror frame. Use one of them "as is" for the backing; cut an oval in the other as shown for the mirror front.

6 Cut a piece of ⅛-inch hardboard (F) to fit between the plywood panels. Cut out the center

of the hardboard to accommodate a 22x48x⅛-inch mirror. Use paneling adhesive to glue the hardboard and mirror between the plywood panels.

7 Fill all exposed plywood edges and sand smooth. Paint the mirror frame as desired. When the paint is dry, hang the frame on the previously assembled stand with conduit hangers.

Materials: ⅜-inch plywood, ⅛-inch hardboard, mirror, 1x6 lumber, ½-inch metal rod, conduit hangers, paneling adhesive, screws, nails, polyurethane varnish, and paint.

FOLDAWAY DESK AND SHELVES

This novel study/hobby center has a lot of things going for it. Your kids will love it because it's just right for studying and other "more enjoyable" pursuits. Besides that, there's plenty of shelving to display all sorts of things. You'll appreciate it for its economy—one sheet of plywood and a few other inexpensive materials are all you need.

1 If you plan to duplicate the pattern shown here, transfer the design (full size) to tracing paper, then to the plywood sheet (A). Or you can create a design of your own, scale it on graph paper, and go from there. Remember, though, that the table surface should be 24 inches from the floor. (Note: You'll want the overall height of the unit to measure slightly less than the height of the ceiling to enable you to position it easily.)

2 Pre-drill a small hole at the starting point. Then, using a saber saw blade with a splinter guard attachment, slowly begin cutting. Keep the speed down as you follow contours and curves to ensure smooth cuts.

3 When all pieces are cut, sand and fill all exposed raw edges with wood filler. Then fasten two 1x2s (B) to the back side of the plywood. Sink nailheads and fill with wood filler. Apply two coats of alkyd-base paint—either gloss or semigloss.

4 Attach the desk top and the shelves plus all of the supports with cut-to-size sections of continuous hinge. Use a hacksaw to cut the hinges.

5 Attach locking tabs (C) fashioned from small pieces of plastic as shown. (Drill an off-center hole in each tab and position it so that when rotated it will hold the shelves and desk top shut.)

6 Attach desk/shelf unit to the wall by screwing it to the wall studs, or if needed, use small metal angles. Counterbore the screws, fill with wood filler, and touch up with paint.

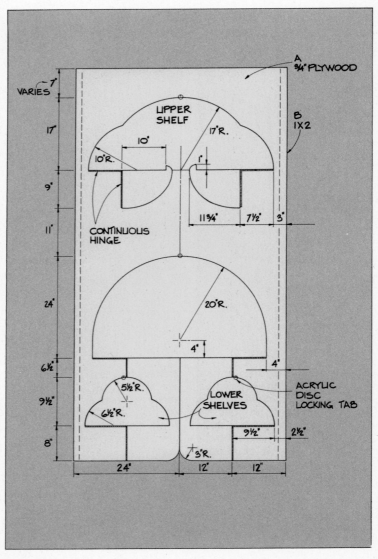

Materials: ¾-inch A-A interior plywood, 1x2 lumber, plastic locking tabs, continuous hinge, glue, nails, screws (or if necessary, small metal angles), wood filler, and paint.

ANYTIME FUN CENTER

This exciting activity panel will captivate your youngsters. Each "cell" has something different happening—blackboard surfaces to write on, plenty of pegboard for prized possessions, shelves for toy storage, and corkboard for pinups.

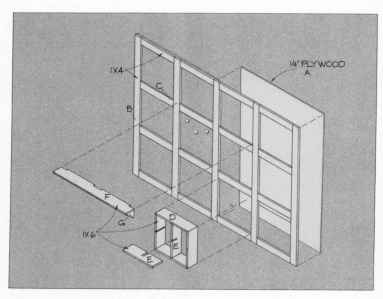

1 Size the unit to fit whatever space is available. The project shown measures 96x72 inches.

2 Cut ¼-inch plywood backing sheets (A) to size.

3 Glue the 1x4 verticals (B) and crosspieces (C) to the backing. Position the center vertical so that it rests on the joint line of the backing sheets.

4 Make a boxlike storage shelf frame from mitered 1x6s (D). Dado the inside surfaces of the 1x6s to accept the center dividers (E). Glue and nail the frame together.

5 Cut the 1x6 dividers (E) to size, notch them as shown in the sketch, and insert them into the 1x6 frame. Then, working from the back side of the wall panel, drive screws into the 1x6 frame members.

6 Cut a long 1x6 shelf (F), notching it as shown to fit around the verticals. Fashion shelf supports (G) from scrap lumber. Nail and glue the shelf to the supports, then screw them to the activity board from behind.

7 Varnish or paint all of the wood surfaces that will be exposed. Screw knobs to backing sheets.

8 Fill in squares as desired. Before inserting the pegboard panel, glue shims to the ¼-inch plywood panel (A) to allow room for hanging the pegboard hardware. Nail the entire unit to the wall studs.

Materials: ¼-inch plywood, 1x6 and 1x4 lumber, pegboard, corkboard, vinyl blackboard wall covering, wooden knobs, glue, nails, screws, and paint or varnish.

BEDSIDE TABLE AND CLOTHES TREE

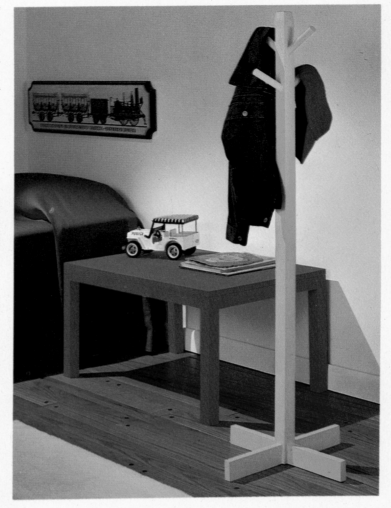

Take a few hours this weekend to delight your kids by knocking together these two bright room additions. You'll be done and ready to paint them before the glue dries.

1 The table measures 17½x30x 16 inches. Build the clothes tree at least four feet tall.

2 Cut 2x2 table legs (A) and the other frame members (B,C). Drill holes and insert ½-inch dowels to assemble (see detail); glue together.

3 Cut lengths of 1x4 (D) for the top. Butt one against the next, gluing and nailing each member to the frame.

4 Sink the nailheads, fill with wood putty, and paint the table as desired.

5 Cut the 2x2 clothes tree pole (E) to length. Taper its top and sand. Cut two ¾x2½-inch-deep notches in the bottom of the 2x2 (see sketch).

6 For the base (F), cut two 18-inch lengths of 1x3. Cut 1¼-inch-deep notches in the center of each. Glue and nail together the members.

7 Attach the base to the clothes tree pole with glue.

8 Drill angled holes near the top of the pole to accommodate ¾-inch dowels (G). Insert five-inch-long dowels, using glue to help hold them in place.

9 Paint the clothes tree.

Materials: (for both the table and the clothes tree): 2x2, 1x4, and 1x3 lumber, ½- and ¾-inch dowels, glue, nails, wood putty, and paint.

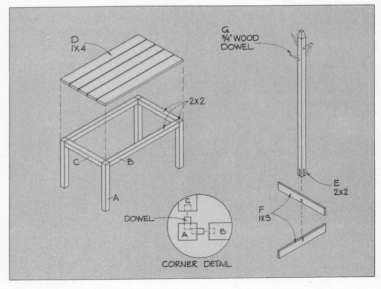

STACKABLE CHEST OF DRAWERS

Furniture in baby's room needs to be bright and cheery—and tough, too. These drawer units stack up to the task admirably with their color-ful yet rugged finish. And you'll love their versatility. Build as many units as you need, and pile them one, two, three, or four high. They're extra roomy.

1 Both the one-drawer and two-drawer units have the same outer dimensions: 32x18x12 inches tall. Build drawers to fit, allowing 1/16-inch tolerance around the drawer fronts.

2 Form the shell for the large drawer unit from 3/4-inch plywood (A,B,C). Glue and nail the members together.

3 Miter 1x3s (D,E) and assemble with glue and nails. Attach to box with glue and nails.

4 Cut the back (F), sides (G), and front (H) from 3/4-inch ply-wood. When cutting the drawer front, allow 1/2 inch on both sides for drawer guides. Rabbet the sides and back to accommodate the 1/4-inch plywood bottom (I). Cut a semicircular drawer pull on front. Assemble the drawer with glue and nails.

5 Attach drawer guides to draw-er and frame.

6 Use a similar procedure to assemble the 3/4-inch plywood shell for the two-drawer unit. Add a center divider (J).

7 Assemble two drawers as be-fore from 3/4-inch plywood—sides (K), back (L), and front (M). In-stall a 1/4-inch plywood bottom (I). Attach drawer guide hardware to drawer and frame.

8 Sink all nailheads and fill the recesses with wood putty. Sand and fill all exposed plywood edges. Paint each of the drawer units as desired. When dry, stack units.

Materials: 3/4- and 1/4-inch ply-wood, 1x3 lumber, drawer guide hardware, glue, nails, wood putty, and paint.

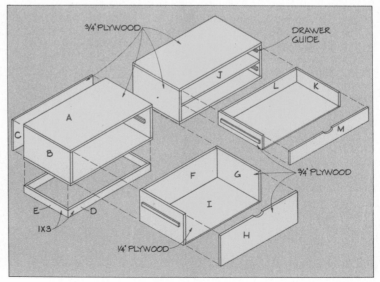

ALL-IN-ONE SOFA UNIT

You'd have to search a store for several pieces of furniture to accomplish everything this inexpensive, do-it-yourself sofa arrangement does. It neatly combines comfortable seating with bonus shelving, plus a couple of swing-up, desk-like end tables.

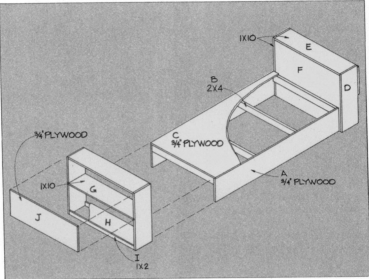

1 Plan to have the seat platform 16 inches from the floor (with cushions). Sofa "arms" are 30 inches high.

2 Cut the sides for the seating platform (A) to size. Sandwich 2x4 stretchers (B) between them; fasten with glue and screws. Using glue and nails, top the frame with a piece of ¾-inch plywood (C).

3 For the bookshelf units, first cut then dado the sides (D) to accept a 1x10 center shelf. Then cut the top (E), back (F), shelves (G,H), and 1x2 stretchers (I) to size. (Rip shelves so they'll fit flush with the sides.)

4 Assemble the bookshelves as shown, using a liberal amount of glue and nails. (Note that the back (F) fits between the sides and beneath the top.)

5 Cut a flip-up top (J) for each of the units. Attach it to the bookshelf with a long continuous hinge. Install locking table leg braces.

6 Fasten the completed bookshelf units to the sofa platform. Drive the screws through the plywood backing into the 2x4 stretchers (B). Sink nailheads, counterbore screwheads, and fill all of the voids with wood putty. Sand and fill all of the exposed plywood edges. Paint the unit as desired. When the finish is dry, add colorful cushions for the sofa seat.

Materials: ¾-inch plywood, 2x4, 1x10, and 1x2 lumber, continuous hinges, locking table leg braces, glue, screws, nails, wood putty, and paint.

BATH AND BEDROOM DRESS-UPS

A little imagination coupled with some basic "how-to" can work wonders when it comes to snazzing up a bath or bedroom. Small do-it-yourself touches such as a handcrafted headboard or a custom-designed shelving arrangement add personality not often matched with store-bought room accessories.

Larger projects such as a complete platform bed ensemble or a self-installed bathroom vanity can save you lots of money, too.

This chapter is packed with ideas, large and small. The projects are designed to be lively yet entirely functional, because in most bedrooms and baths there's not much room to devote to frills.

You'll quickly see that practicality doesn't have to be dull, even when space is a problem. Creative use of color and structure plus a little careful planning can make any of these projects fit your needs beautifully.

Browse through the next few pages and see if they don't trigger some kind of inspiration for your bath or bedroom. You may find the exact fix-up you need!

CUSTOMIZED LOOKING GLASS AND CABINET

This dual project for the bath offers two big advantages over traditional in-wall units. First, you don't have to knock out a hole for installation. Second, the convenient open-shelf cabinet puts toiletries alongside the mirror for easy access on sleepy mornings.

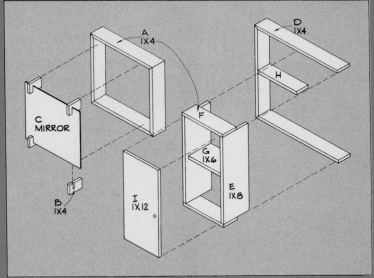

1 Plan dimensions for the mirror and cabinet frames to fit your wall space.

2 Miter four identical lengths of 1×4 (A) to frame mirror. Don't assemble them yet.

3 Cut and notch small sections of 1×4 (B) to hold a ⅛-inch-thick mirror. Glue and nail to two of the frame boards (A).

4 Assemble three sides of the mirror frame with nails and glue.

5 Sink nailheads and fill with wood putty. Paint all pieces of the frame. When dry, insert mirror (C). Glue and nail on fourth side of frame, sinking nailheads and touching up with paint.

6 For the cabinet frame, cut 1×4s (D) to size. Join the mitered ends with glue and nails.

7 For the enclosed portion of the cabinet, rip two 1×8 verticals (E) to a seven-inch width. Nail short 1×4 stretchers (F) to the 1×8s as shown.

8 Install a 1×6 center shelf (G) as shown.

9 Slip the cabinet assembly into the previously assembled outer frame (see step 6) and nail in place. Install 1×4 shelf (H).

10 Sink all nails, fill holes, and paint the cabinet.

11 Rip a 1×12 (I) to fit the cabinet opening. Drill a finger hole or attach a knob. Paint. Hang door with two butt hinges.

12 Attach mirror and cabinet assemblies to wall with small metal angles.

Materials: 1×12, 1×8, 1×6, and 1×4 lumber, ⅛-inch mirror, wood putty, nails, glue, butt hinges, metal angles, and paint.

MARQUEE-STYLE VANITY

A basic black-and-white color scheme and clean lines combine to create the good looks of this easy-to-build bathroom dress-up. But don't let the simplicity fool you. The unit combines a good number of elements—medicine chest, mirror, linen closet, lighting, and vanity.

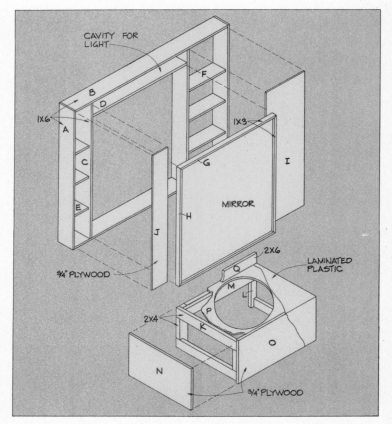

1 Build this project to fit whatever space you have. Figure your outermost dimensions first and adjust the inner measurements to fit.

2 Cut 1×6s (A, B) for the outer frame of the shelving unit. Fasten with glue and screws.

3 Cut the inner 1×6 verticals (C) to size, then secure with screws. Follow by screwing a 1×6 crosspiece (D) in place as shown. Space these members so the fixture you select will fill the cavity you're creating.

4 Cut, then nail shelves (E, F) in place.

5 Sink exposed screwheads and nailheads, and fill with wood putty. Paint the unit.

6 Locate wall studs, then fasten the shelving unit to them with metal angles.

7 Run necessary wiring to accommodate a marquee-style light fixture. Wire the light fixture.

8 Miter-cut 1×3s (G, H) for the mirror frame. (Size the members so the frame will fit snugly in the cavity below the fixture.) Dado the inside surface of each member to accommodate a ¼-inch mirror. Paint the frame.

9 Assemble three sides of the mirror frame with glue and nails and slide the mirror in place. Glue and nail on the fourth side of the frame. Fasten the framed mirror to the shelving unit. Sink all nails, fill with putty, and touch up with paint.

10 Cut out doors (I, J) for the shelf sections from ¾-inch plywood. Fill edges with wood putty, then paint, hinge, and install the doors.

11 If necessary, rough in plumbing for the lavatory. Then, construct a frame for the sink unit from 2×4s (K, L, M) as shown. Using lag screws, anchor the frame securely to at least two wall studs.

12 Sheathe the sides of the frame with ¾-inch plywood (N, O). Cut a top panel (P) for the vanity. Nail in place.

13 Nail a 2×6 to the wall studs to serve as a backsplash (Q).

14 Cover the exposed surfaces of the vanity and backsplash with laminate (see page 83).

15 Cut a hole in the countertop, install the sink, and connect the plumbing lines.

Materials: ¾-inch plywood, 2×4, 1×6, 2×6, and 1×3 lumber, mirror, light fixture, electrical supplies, metal angles, screws, glue, nails, wood putty, paint, plastic laminate, and adhesive.

LAMINATED STORE-ALL AND VANITY

If you're sitting there saying, "I couldn't make something that looks as custom-made as that," you'd better look again. The cabinetmaker look of this handsome bathroom duo is achieved with 1×3 finish-grade lumber and simple joinery techniques.

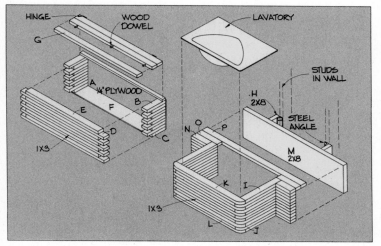

1 To build the storage unit, cut a piece of ¼-inch plywood to serve as the back (A).

2 Cut enough long (B) and short (C) sections of 1×3 to form the sides. Short sections will be 2½ inches shorter than the longer ones. Alternating long and short lengths, assemble each side by gluing and nailing together.

3 Cut long and short 1×3s (D, E) for the front of the unit. Measure carefully. Alternating lengths as before, glue and nail together.

4 Glue ends of members, then finger-join the side assemblies to the front assembly. Round the edges; sand smooth.

5 Cut a ¼-inch plywood bottom (F). Secure with nails to the 1×3s. Nail and glue the plywood back to the 1×3s.

6 Fashion the unit's lid (G) with more 1×3s. Edge-join the 1×3s using glue and clamps. Hinge the lid and connect it to a ripped

1×3 fastened as shown.

7 Sink exposed nailheads and fill with wood putty. Apply two coats of polyurethane varnish. When dry, screw the storage unit to the wall at desired height.

8 For the vanity, attach 2×8 spacers (H) to wall studs with sturdy metal angles (see sketch).

9 Cut alternating lengths of 1×3s for the sides (I, J) and front (K, L) of the vanity frame. Glue and nail together as before.

10 Screw and glue a 2×8 back (M) to the vanity frame. Anchor the unit to the wall by gluing and screwing securely through the back into the spacers. Glue and nail 1×3 trim strips (N, O, P).

11 Apply two coats of polyurethane varnish. Install lavatory.

Materials: ¼-inch plywood, 2×8 and 1×3 lumber, metal angles, screws, nails, wood putty, glue, and polyurethane varnish.

BUILD-IN
SHELVING
ALCOVE

Here's a project that looks like a tricky remodeling job but isn't. Just build a 2×4 frame, cover with drywall, paint, and install the shelving. You'll be amazed with the results!

1 Build this shelving enclosure so its sides extend about 10 inches out into the room. Measure floor to ceiling to figure your vertical dimensions.

2 Construct the 2×4 stub walls (A, B) as shown.

3 Position the walls and nail to the wall, floor, and ceiling.

4 Tie the walls together by toenailing the 2×6s (C) in place.

5 Sheathe all of the framing with drywall. Use perforated tape and joint compound to hide seams and nailheads. Nail lengths of metal bead to the outside corners for protection.

6 Apply a primer/sealer and, when dry, paint the enclosure.

7 Fasten a piece of paneling to the wall (D) to form a background for the shelves. Glue the panel in place using a good paneling adhesive.

8 Secure adjustable shelf supports to the inside walls of the enclosure as shown.

9 Install ³⁄₁₆-inch-thick tempered glass shelves with sealed edges cut to size at desired intervals.

Materials: 2×4 and 2×6 lumber, ½-inch drywall, paneling, paneling adhesive, perforated tape, metal bead, joint compound, shelf standards and clips, ³⁄₁₆-inch-thick tempered glass shelves, primer/sealer, paint, and nails.

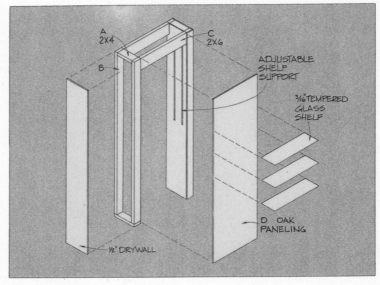

FLIP-TOP CORNER HAMPER

If your bathroom is short on storage space, check to see if you're using every nook and cranny to best advantage.

Chances are there's a vacant corner where you can suspend a simple clothes hamper like the one shown here.

1 This is a free-form-design project—choose the size and shape you need to fit your exact situation. Build it big enough to be useful, yet small enough to be out of the way. One caution: Because of its shape, you'll need to figure angles carefully to get a good fit at the corners.

2 Use ¾-inch interior plywood for the construction. Cut the back (A) and the sides (B, C, D) first, mitering the edges as necessary to ensure snug joints at the corners of the unit.

3 Glue and nail the back and sides together. Then, using the assembly as a pattern, cut out the bottom (E) and top (F). Attach bottom. Sink all nailheads and fill with wood putty.

4 For a durable surface, apply plastic laminate to the sides, top, and all exposed edges (see page 83). Or, if desired, paint all surfaces with two coats of a good quality interior alkyd-base paint. In either case, be sure that you paint the inside surfaces of the box, too.

5 When finishing is complete and paint is dry, attach the top using two butt hinges, or if desired, a piano hinge.

6 Attach the unit to a wall. Predrill holes and screw from the inside of the hamper directly into at least two wall studs. Use toggle bolts, too, if necessary for a secure hold.

Materials: ¾-inch plywood, plastic laminate and adhesive, two butt hinges (or one piano hinge), wood putty, paint, glue, nails, and screws.

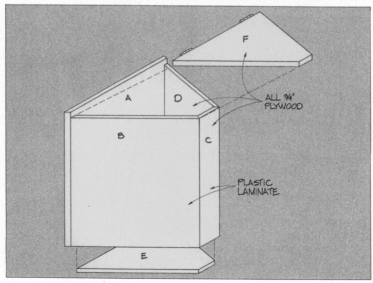

REDWOOD TUB SURROUND

Redwood or cedar paneling offers a refreshing break from the traditional enamel-and-tile bathroom fare. But be sure to seal each board with several coats of polyurethane varnish to prevent discoloration from normal bathroom moisture.

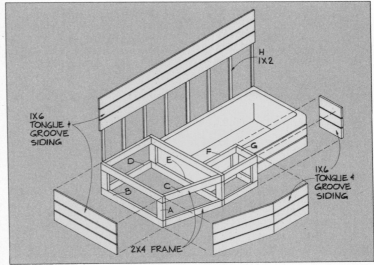

1 Tailor this project to the size of your tub and the space available. You can build the tub deck to serve only as a wrap-around platform, or large enough to function as a bench as well. You'll find it helpful to plan your strategy on graph paper before beginning construction.

2 Assemble the frame for the deck from 2×4 verticals (A) and crosspieces (B, C, D, E, F, G). Miter the crosspieces for the angled side as necessary.

3 Rough in necessary plumbing.

4 Attach 1×2 furring strips (H) to the wall (extend them to the ceiling).

5 Cover the deck top and sides with 1×6 tongue-and-groove redwood or cedar, bedding the joints in caulk to repel water. Leave openings for plumbing fixtures as necessary. Miter the boards wherever necessary to achieve a good fit. Use paneling adhesive to attach siding directly to the sides of the tub. (If your tub is the curved type, even the surface with 1×2s and shims.)

6 Nail siding to furring strips to cover the wall.

7 Apply two or three coats of polyurethane to the siding. Allow time between coats for the finish to dry. When the last coat has dried, complete the plumbing installations.

8 Caulk around edges of the siding and fixtures wherever moisture could be a problem.

Materials: 2×4 and 1×2 lumber, 1×6 tongue-and-groove redwood or cedar siding, paneling adhesive, caulk, nails, polyurethane varnish, and plumbing accessories.

68

ROOM DIVIDER DUO

Sometimes, just a little privacy is all you need—enough to disguise a sleeping area or to break the monotony of a long, narrow room. This simple-to-build divider and plant stand combo will do either effectively and inexpensively.

1 Build the screen panels seven feet high and as wide as you need them; the plant stand can be any height that suits your purposes.

2 Cut each screen panel from ¾-inch A-A plywood.

3 Apply wood veneer tape to cover the "raw" exposed edges of each panel. Then finish the panels as desired. A couple of coats of polyurethane varnish will protect the panel surfaces.

4 Fasten the screen panels together with double-action hinges—three hinges between each pair of panels. If you build more than six panel sections, use four hinges between each pair of panels to prevent binding.

5 Build the plant stand from 1×12s that match the veneer used for the folding screen. Cut four identically sized pieces for the sides. For a professional job, miter along the length of each board as shown and glue and nail together.

6 Sink nailheads and fill the holes with wood putty. Apply a finish that matches or complements the divider panels.

Materials: ¾-inch plywood, 1× 12 lumber, double-action hinges, wood veneer tape, nails, glue, and the finish of your choice.

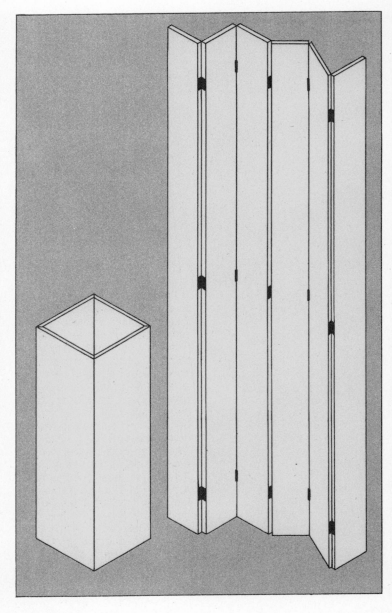

LATTICEWORK WALL-WINDOW TREATMENT

Add a little cheer to a lackluster bedroom with this colorful, easy-build fix-up. Size it to dramatize a whole wall, or if that's a bit too much cheer for you, use it to accent a window. Either way, you'll fill the room with a rainbow of color.

1 Measure from floor to ceiling to figure vertical dimensions. If you're building this project around a window, make the width slightly wider than the outside dimensions of the window.

2 Cut 2×6 verticals (A) to size. Nail a 1×6 header (B) between the verticals. Complete the frame with a base panel cut from ½-inch plywood (C). Sink nailheads and fill with wood putty.

3 Drill holes in the 1×6 header.

4 Cut lattice strips (D) to size. Drill holes in each (see photo).

5 Paint the frame and individual lattice strips as desired. When dry, attach the frame to floor and ceiling with metal angles.

6 "String" lattice strips one from the other using binder rings as shown. Hang each series of strips from the 1×6 header.

Materials: ½-inch plywood, 2×6 and 1×6 lumber, lattice strips, binder rings, nails, wood putty, and paint.

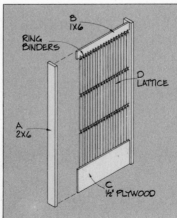

DESIGNER HEADBOARD ENSEMBLE

This headboard/shelving creation is a dramatic example of how color and texture can combine to produce an impressive decorating effect. Here, both the headboard fabric and the shelving uprights take their cues from the bed linens. You'll find this project a winning—and pennywise—substitute for the more traditional headboard options.

1 Measure floor to ceiling to figure the length of the 2×2 uprights (A). Select a fabric panel (B) that's two to three inches wider than your bed.

2 Cut the uprights to size, then paint them. Tack or staple the fabric panel to the back of two uprights, fasten one of these to the wall, stretch the fabric tight, and nail the other upright to the wall. Sink nailheads, fill with wood putty, and touch up with paint.

3 Install a row of mirror tiles next to each upright. Follow by attaching two more uprights to flank the mirror tiles.

4 Measure the width of a mirror tile to position the remaining two groups of 2×2s. Toenail each to floor and ceiling.

5 Install glass shelves using metal angles as shelf supports.

Materials: 2×2 lumber, fabric, ¼-inch tempered glass, metal angles, nails, wood putty, paint.

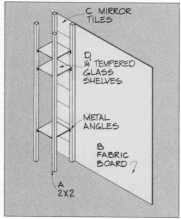

C MIRROR TILES

D ¼" TEMPERED GLASS SHELVES

METAL ANGLES

B FABRIC BOARD

A 2×2

DOUBLE-DUTY DESK

When bedroom space is a problem, this roomy desk is the answer. Place it at either the head or foot of your bed. With the handy built-in shelf, you'll eliminate the need for an adjacent night table.

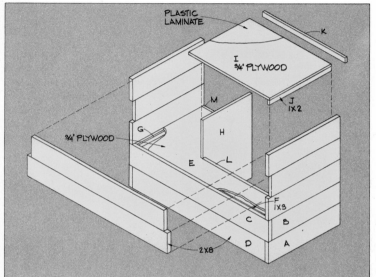

1 Standard desk height is 30 inches, so plan your vertical dimensions accordingly. Figure all other measurements to suit your needs (position the built-in shelf slightly above mattress level).

2 Cut 2×8s for the sides (A, B) and back (C, D). Note the alternating long/short construction. Skip a board where you want to locate the shelf. Glue and screw the 2×8s together, counterboring screwheads. Fill with wood putty or dowel plugs.

3 Cut an L-shaped shelf (E) from ¾-inch plywood. Nail on 1×2 support ledgers (F, G) as shown in the sketch. Apply plastic laminate to the shelf top (see page 83). Position the shelf so it is flush with the bottom of the opening that will face the bed. Nail and glue in place.

4 Cut a vertical divider (H) from ¾-inch plywood. (This piece also helps to support the desk.) Glue and nail it to the center shelf (E).

5 Cut another piece of plywood to serve as the desk top (I). Install a 1×2 support ledger (J). Glue and nail the desk top to the ledger and the previously installed center support (F). Apply plastic laminate to top.

6 Trim the front edge of the desk top with a 1×3 (K). Also add 1×3 trim (L, M) to the exposed edges of the center shelf.

7 Apply two coats polyurethane varnish to exposed surfaces.

Materials: ¾-inch plywood, 2×8, 1×3, and 1×2 lumber, plastic laminate and adhesive, polyurethane varnish, wood putty, nails, screws, and glue.

SPACE-SAVER MINI-OFFICE

This compact work center solves problems in limited-space situations. It features a simple desk/bookshelf combo that's a snap to knock togeth-er. And as a bonus, the matching storage cube mounts on casters for roll-around convenience. Perfect for that small extra bedroom!

1 Adjust the size of the project to suit the space available. Keep in mind that standard desk height is 30 inches.

2 Cut two identical lengths of ¾-inch plywood (A) for the bookshelf. Butt them together as shown and attach with glue and nails. Strengthen the assembly with triangular plywood gussets (B); attach them with glue and nails.

3 The desk is an upside-down version of the bookshelf. Cut two large, identical sections of ¾-inch plywood (C) and butt together with glue and nails. Fasten braces (D).

4 Cut out pieces for the storage cube from ¾-inch plywood: sides (E), back (F), and top and bottom (G). Note that the sides (E) are angled at the top. Before assembling, cut a ¼-inch-deep dado on the inside surface of each side (E) to accommodate a ⅛-inch hardboard shelf (H).

5 Assemble the cube with glue and nails. Install shelf (H).

6 Cut and assemble mitered 1×2s (I, J) to form a base for the unit. Glue and nail to the bottom of the cube.

7 Screw four plate casters to the bottom of the storage cube.

8 Sink all nailheads, fill them and all plywood edges with wood putty, and paint the desk, bookshelf, and storage unit. If desired, cover desk top with plastic laminate (see page 83).

Materials: ¾-inch plywood, 1×2 lumber, ⅛-inch hardboard, glue, nails, paint, and four plate casters.

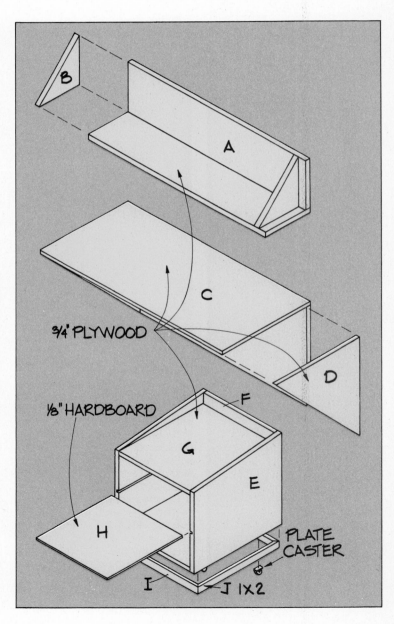

WRAP-AROUND HEADBOARD/ STORAGE UNIT

With drawer space to spare and an abundance of up-top shelf area, too, this good-looking U-shaped headboard and night table arrangement offers a welcome end to bedside clutter. It can be built at a price you can afford.

1 Build this project so its top surface exceeds the height of your bed by about 15 inches. Make the "headboard" two inches longer than the bed's width.

2 Build the headboard "box" from ¾-inch plywood. Butt together two pieces (A, B) and fasten with glue and nails. Cap each end with plywood (C).

3 Assemble the shelving unit without drawers from ¾-inch plywood. Cut top and bottom panels (D) and butt them against front and back panels (E) as shown. Add a vertical divider (same as E); then, install a center shelf (G) in each compartment. Nail side panels (F) in place.

4 For the combination drawer and shelving unit, cut ¾-inch plywood top and bottom panels (H), side panels (I, J) and back panel (K). Glue and nail these pieces together as shown.

5 Fit a vertical divider (L) into the cabinet. Add a center shelf (M).

6 Construct drawers from ½-inch plywood, butting the back (N) and bottom (O) between side panels (P). Size the drawers to accommodate the guide hardware. Glue and nail together. Nail on the drawer fronts (Q) and attach drawer pulls.

7 Install the drawer guides and pulls.

8 Bolt the headboard assembly between the two shelving units.

9 Sink all nailheads and fill with wood putty. Paint.

Materials: ¾-inch and ½-inch plywood, drawer guides, drawer pulls, screws, nuts and bolts, nails, glue, and paint.

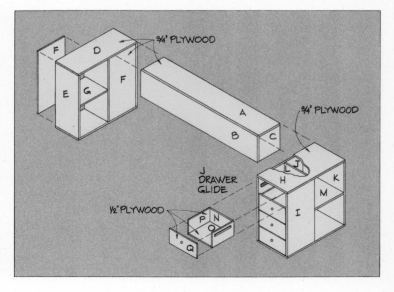

MATCH-MATE BOOKSHELF

Here's a simple bookshelf that's every bit as attractive as the headboard it adorns. You can accent any store-bought headboard this way—just style the shelf supports along the same lines as the headboard, and paint or stain to match. Your bookshelf will look like an original part of the bed set.

1 Cut the 1×10 shelf (A) to size—headboard wide or wider; then, cut a 1×4 support ledger (B) to the same length. Butt one to the other as shown, gluing and nailing together. Add a 1×2 (C) along the front edge.

2 Trace patterns on a 1×10 for the shelf supports (E). Cut trim strips (F, G) from another section of 1×10. Glue and nail the shelf support assemblies together.

3 Attach shelf supports to the bookshelf assembly (A, B, C). Cap ends with short 2×2s (D).

4 Sink nailheads and fill with wood putty. Paint or stain.

Materials: 2×2, 1×10, 1×4, and 1×2 lumber, glue, wood putty, nails, and paint or stain.

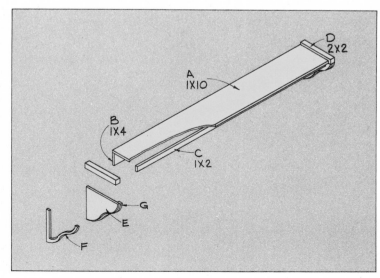

KING-SIZE PLATFORM BED ENSEMBLE

1 Adapt the construction shown to fit any size bed. Build as many bookshelf tiers as you need for bedside convenience.

2 Cut lengths of ¾-inch plywood (A, B) to form the boxlike frame for the platform. Butt the ends and screw together. Counterbore screwheads and fill with wood putty or dowel plugs.

3 Nail 2×4 stretchers (C) and a 2×6 center support (D) to the inside of the frame as shown in the sketch. Recess each stretcher ¾ inch to accommodate the platform top (E). Nail the plywood top panels to the stretchers.

4 Give the entire platform assembly two coats of paint.

5 Miter 1×3 boards (F,G) to form sides for the bookshelves. Cut a ¼-inch rabbet on the top inside surface of each to accommodate the ¼-inch plywood shelf panel (H). Use nails and glue to assemble each bookshelf. Sink all nailheads and fill the recesses with wood putty.

6 Attach shelf standards to the wall. Use eight-inch-long shelf brackets to support each of the bookshelves.

7 (Optional) Drill holes in the top bookshelf assemblies to accept a two-inch pipe (I) for hanging cushioned headboard panels as shown.

8 Paint the bookshelves to match the bed platform.

Materials: ¾-inch plywood, ¼-inch plywood, 2×6, 2×4, and 1×3 lumber, shelf standards and brackets, 2-inch-diameter pipe (optional), nails, glue, wood putty, and paint.

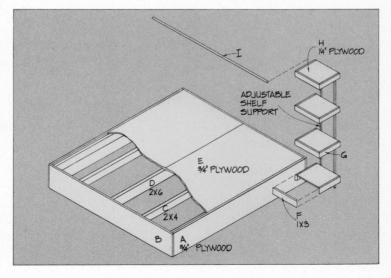

PLANNING AND BUILDING BASICS

Have you ever heard the saying, "It's not hard once you know how to do it"? Well it's true, especially when it comes to building projects for your home. Once you've mastered the basics, each project you do becomes a series of accomplishable steps rather than a major undertaking.

So, do yourself a favor and spend a few minutes learning about the steppingstones to professional-looking projects. It'll be worth your while.

COMMON CONSTRUCTION MATERIALS

The materials you use for construction will vary, depending on the item's intended use. So when making your selection, ask yourself these questions: Are you constructing something for indoor or outdoor use? Is the item strictly utilitarian, or will it be suitable for use in a living room? Is it intended for light-duty use, or will it be a long-lived project subject to considerable use—and abuse?

Hardboard

Hardboard is available in 4x8-foot sheets and comes in ⅛- and ¼-inch thicknesses. Standard hardboard is an excellent choice for cabinetwork, drawer bottoms, and concealed panels.

You can also get hardboard perforated with holes spaced about one inch apart. Perforated hardboard is recommended for building storage for soiled laundry and for the backs of hi-fi cabinets. The quarter- and eighth-inch perforated hardboard lends itself to storing garden equipment and tools, too, as its holes accept hooks designed for this purpose. To expand or change the arrangement, just switch the hooks around. If the project will be subject to dampness, use tempered hardboard.

Particle board, chip board, and flake board, also members of the hardboard family, have a coarser grain structure, are lighter in color, and are available in thicknesses up to ¾ inch. These products are made of granulated or shredded wood particles forced together under pressure with a binder at high temperatures.

Plywood

Plywood also comes in 4x8-foot sheets, though larger sheets are available on special order. Thicknesses range from ⅛-inch to ¾-inch. For light-duty storage, the ¼- and ½-inch thicknesses are adequate. If you are planning to build an outdoor storage unit, specify *exterior grade* when making your purchase. Exterior grade plywood has its layers glued together with a waterproof glue to withstand rain.

The surfaces of plywood sheets are graded A, B, C, and D—with A the smoother, better surface and D the least desirable appearance. Choose AA (top grade, both sides) only for projects where both sides will be exposed; use a less expensive combination for others.

Solid Wood

Plain, ordinary wood still ranks as the most popular building material. Wood is sold by the "board foot" (1x12x12 inches). One board foot equals the surface area of one square foot, with a nominal thickness of one inch.

Wood is marketed by "grade." For most building projects No. 2 grade will satisfy your needs. This grade may have some blemishes, such as loose knots, but these don't reduce the strength of the wood.

If you're planning to build a unit that will be part of a room's decor, you should buy *select lumber*—a grade that's relatively free of blemishes.

Remember, too, that outdoor projects are a different subject. Redwood or cedar is preferable, but if you use a soft wood, be sure to treat it for moisture resistance. Or buy pressure-treated wood.

You can buy boards up to 16 feet in length and 12 inches in width, though occasionally a lumberyard may have somewhat wider or longer boards.

Wood is divided into two categories. Softwoods, used commonly for general construction, come from trees that don't shed their leaves in the winter: hemlock, fir, pine, spruce, and similar evergreen cone-bearing trees. Hardwoods come from trees that do shed their leaves: maple, oak, birch, mahogany, walnut, and other broad-leaved varieties.

All lumber is sold by a nominal size. A 2x4, for example, does not measure two by four inches. It's actually 1½x3½ inches (though the nominal *length* of a 2x4 is usually its true length). The drawing shows nominal sizes, as well as the actual sizes, of most pieces of common lumber.

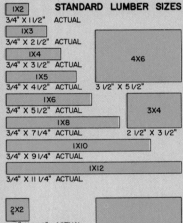

STANDARD LUMBER SIZES

1X2 — 3/4" X 1 1/2" ACTUAL
1X3 — 3/4" X 2 1/2" ACTUAL
1X4 — 3/4" X 3 1/2" ACTUAL
1X5 — 3/4" X 4 1/2" ACTUAL
1X6 — 3/4" X 5 1/2" ACTUAL
1X8 — 3/4" X 7 1/4" ACTUAL
1X10 — 3/4" X 9 1/4" ACTUAL
1X12 — 3/4" X 11 1/4" ACTUAL

4X6 — 3 1/2" X 5 1/2"
3X4 — 2 1/2" X 3 1/2"

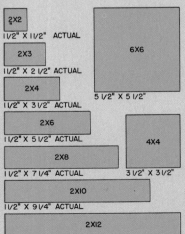

2X2 — 1 1/2" X 1 1/2" ACTUAL
2X3 — 1 1/2" X 2 1/2" ACTUAL
2X4 — 1 1/2" X 3 1/2" ACTUAL
2X6 — 1 1/2" X 5 1/2" ACTUAL
2X8 — 1 1/2" X 7 1/4" ACTUAL
2X10 — 1 1/2" X 9 1/4" ACTUAL
2X12 — 1 1/2" X 11 1/4" ACTUAL

6X6 — 5 1/2" X 5 1/2"
4X4 — 3 1/2" X 3 1/2"

HOW TO MAXIMIZE A CLOSET

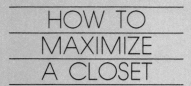

Getting More Into a Shallow Closet

Shallow bedroom closets offer lots of room for improvement. With most, you get a single pole, a shelf, and bypass doors.

Start your analysis of a closet's efficiency with the doors. If both

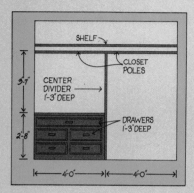

sides of your closet are often in use, you may want to replace awkward sliding panels with a set of bifold units.

Next, study how space is used inside. Group garments by size and you'll probably discover a sizable open space under the shorter items. A second closet pole halfway down will help here.

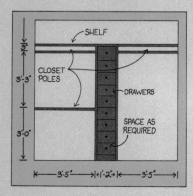

Both of the designs shown above put the space in shallow closets to better use. The first, which works with either bypass or bifold doors, includes a draw-

er case, which takes pressure off freestanding storage elsewhere. The second design features two rods on one side for shorter clothes. With it, you need bifolds. Shelves may be substituted for the drawers in either closet. (The spaces allowed for hanging clothes are minimums.)

Getting More Into a Walk-in Closet

Walk-in closets, though usually larger than their shallow cousins, provide less storage space per square foot. Subtract the minimum two-foot-wide corridor for access and you can see why.

Install closet poles along the longer wall or walls. Double-tiered poles for suits, skirts, and other shorter items can give you half again as much hanging space. Purchased items can expand storage, too. Don't overlook old standbys like shoe racks and coat hooks, as well as the newer closet "shelving systems" marketed by some manufacturers.

Shelves—either at the back or along one wall—often will hold all of your folded clothes. It's best to space them about seven inches apart to minimize rummaging.

Check out the shelf possibilities above the closet poles for storing seasonal or seldom-worn clothing. Install a second shelf 12 inches above the existing one and you won't have to stack boxes on top of one another.

Getting More Into a Linen Closet

The solution for this often jumbled closet is to compartmentalize. Check the following drawing to see one scheme for putting foldables in their places. Blankets go up top, then bath towels, sheets, hand towels, and so on.

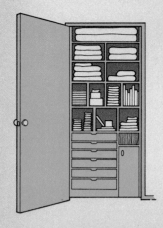

Plan your divisions according to the things you have and the way you fold them, leaving some clearance for getting them in and out. Don't over-engineer, though. Be sure to allow for the thickness of shelves and dividers.

Dimensions You Need to Know

You'll be wise to become familiar with a few basic measurements before you take on any linen or clothes closet reorganization. Closet poles normally are hung 12 to 14 inches from the wall, but in a tight situation you could cut this distance to 10 inches. The two tables shown list other dimensions for linens and clothes.

Linen Closet Items

Pillowcases	7×15″
Blankets	27×22½″
Sheets	
Flat	13½×15″
Fitted	18×10½″
Washcloths	7×7″
Hand Towels	6×10″
Bath Towels	14×13″
Bath Mats	10×9″
Dish Towels	10×16″

(Maximum Space Requirements—Folded)

Clothes Closet Paraphernalia

Women's Items		Men's Items		Accessories	
Long dresses	69″	Topcoats	50″	Garment bags	57″
Robes	52″	Suits	38″	Hanging shoe bags	36″
Skirts	35″	Travel bags	41″	Umbrellas	36″
Dresses	45″	Trousers (cuff-hung)	44″	Canes	36″
Dress bags	48″	Trousers			
Blouses	28″	(double-hung)	20″		
Coats	52″	Ties	27″		
Suits	29″	Shirts	28″		
Suit bags	41″				

HOW TO TILE BATHROOM WALLS

Tiling a bathroom or shower area need not be an overwhelming task. Take your time and plan carefully, and you'll be rewarded with a tough surface that will last for years.

Figuring Tile Needs

To piece together a smooth installation you'll need two different types of tiles. Field tiles (4¼-and 6-inch squares are typical sizes) cover most of the surface; trim tiles round off edges and get around corners.

Small mosaic tiles come bonded to pieces of 1×1- or 1×2-foot paper or fabric mesh; they go up quickly, but require more grout.

Pre-grouted tile sheets include 4¼-inch tiles and flexible synthetic grouting; you cement the sheets to the wall, then seal edges with a caulking gun.

To compute how many field tiles you'll need for an entire bathroom, draw each wall on graph paper, count the squares, and add about five percent for waste. Or simply calculate the square footage and let your dealer do the figuring.

In a shower, plan to tile to a height of at least six inches above the shower head. Other bathroom walls usually are tiled to the four-foot level.

Estimate trim tiles such as bullnoses, caps, and coves by the lineal foot; order mitered corners, angles, and other specialty items by the piece. Don't get carried away with a low price per square foot for field tiles until you've checked out what the trim tiles will cost. These can add substantially to the final bill.

For adhesive, choose an organic "Type I" for shower-tub areas and other wet locations, and "Type II" for walls that remain relatively dry. One gallon covers about 50 square feet.

Dry-mix grout usually comes in five-pound bags. One bag will grout 100 square feet of 4¼-inch tiles, or approximately 15 square feet of mosaics.

Tools for Tile Work

Many tile dealers rent specialized equipment on a per-day basis. But because a good job can take a surprising amount of time, plan first to set all the tiles that don't have to be cut, then rent the cutter and nippers you'll need for trimming.

A tile-cutter cuts accurate, straight lines quickly. Ask your dealer for a demonstration—and expect to ruin a few tiles before you get the hang of it. Nippers nibble out curved cuts.

The serrated edges of notched trowels let you spread adhesive to just the right thickness; small notched spreaders get into tight spots.

A rubber float facilitates grouting, but you can get by with an ordinary window washer's squeegee.

Preparing Walls For Tile

You can apply ceramic tile to any drywall, plaster, or plywood surface that is smooth, sound, and firm. With existing walls, strip wallpaper and scrape away loose paint. Knock the sheen from glossy finishes with a light sanding.

Don't bother taping and smoothing joints in new drywall. Seal it first, however, with a thin coat of adhesive, taking care to pack all openings where pipes come through. In a shower or other high-moisture location, use special water-resistant drywall or exterior-grade plywood.

Pay particular attention to the point where tile will meet the top of a tub or shower base. Chip away any old material and leave a ¼-inch space. After tiling, seal with caulking compound.

Laying Field Tiles

Now you're ready to begin laying out the job. The following drawings show how to establish guidelines for an installation that starts in the center of a wall and proceeds toward the edges. This method gives you equally sized cut tiles at each side. If that's not important, start in a corner. But check for plumb first; you may have to trim some tiles.

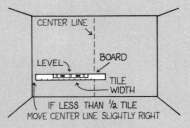

Improvise a layout tool by fastening a level to a straight board. Then mark off tile widths, including ¹⁄₁₆-inch grouting. Mark a plumb line at the wall's midpoint. Now use your guide to see what will happen at the edges. Shift the field if necessary.

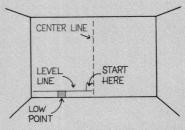

Finally, find the wall's lowest point. Mark a level line one tile width above it. Begin setting full tiles above this line.

The field tiles that cover the body of the wall go up quickly. Set all of them before trimming and fitting around edges, pipes, and fixtures.

Apply the adhesive in two- to three-square-foot sections until you get a feel for setting the tiles. Caution: Most adhesives give off toxic fumes; provide ventilation.

Spread adhesive with the trowel's notched edge, combing it out in beaded lines. Spaces between the lines should be almost bare. Set the first few full tiles in place. Use a slight twist, but don't slide them. Maintain about ¹⁄₁₆ inch between tiles for grout. After you've checked to see that a tile is square with its neighbors and is properly spaced, press it firmly into the adhesive. If adhesive oozes from beneath the tile, you're applying too much. Use a toothpick to clean out excess adhesive before it dries.

Cutting and Fitting

After all the field tiles are up (be sure to leave space for soap dishes and other accessories), begin filling in the edges. Expect slow going here, especially at first when you have to master the knack of fracturing tiles.

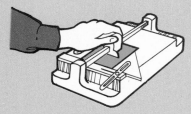

To trim tile with a tile cutter, bear down heavily and score with a single, even line. Then snap the tile with a flick of the handle. If you score tiles with a glass cutter, use a square as a guide. Don't go back over the score or you will get a crumbly break. To break, place the score

over the edge of a board or table, and snap downward. With practice, the tile will break where you want. Smooth rough edges with a wood file or abrasive stone. A file will also cut notches or enlarge bored holes.

To fit tile around a pipe, measure, then cut the tile in two along the pipe's center axis and nibble out semicircular notches from each piece. Smooth the notches

with a file, then cement the pieces in place. After grouting, seal with caulking compound.

Scribe-fit tiles to a tub or other fixture, as shown below. Let the steel point of the compass follow the contour of the fixture. Mark with a pen and cut with nippers. To avoid breaking tiles, start at the edge and bite out tiny chunks.

SET COMPASS TO THIS WIDTH

Install soap dishes and other ceramic accessories last, using adhesive or two-part epoxy putty. Secure them with masking tape until the adhesive or putty dries. Don't use accessories during the two-week curing period.

Grouting

Grouting—the final stage of any tile job—goes fairly quickly. Check with your dealer for the right grout to use with your tile.

Mix grout to the consistency of a thick paste and apply it with diagonal passes of a rubber float, taking care to pack all joints. After 10 to 15 minutes, tool the joints with a rounded object such as the handle of a toothbrush to further compact the grout. Scrub all grout off the tiles with a wet sponge. Finally, polish the tiles with a soft, dry cloth.

Curing

You can speed the curing process of conventional cement-mix grout by misting it with water for three or four days after tile installation. When the grout has thoroughly cured—about two weeks—you can coat it with a special sealer designed to ward off dirt and mildew. Don't use a newly tiled shower for two weeks.

HOW TO LAY CARPETING

Integral-Pad Carpeting

Integral-pad carpeting is the quickest do-it-yourself floor covering of all because it offers one-step installation. Before laying it, all you need to do is remove shoe molding and clean the floor. Then, loosely fit the carpeting, running it slightly up the walls on all sides. Pull tight and trim off excess.

If your room is wider than the carpeting, you'll have to seam together two sections. Use two rows of double-faced carpet tape where seams fall.

Integral-pad carpeting is non-skid; however, if desired, you can add carpet tape or adhesive around the borders.

Jute-Backed Carpeting

This type requires that you install a separate pad beneath the carpeting. First, fasten tackless strips (about ⅜ inch out from the baseboard) around the perimeter of the room; these hold the carpeting tight once stretched.

Next, unroll the padding (there are several types to choose from) and cut it to fit within the borders created by the tackless strips.

Then, unroll the carpeting, maneuver it into position, and smooth it out as best you can. With this out of the way, rough-cut the carpeting so that it laps up onto the walls about two inches all around.

Starting in one corner, stay-tack the goods one foot out from the adjacent walls at about 12-inch intervals. Then move to the other side of the room and starting from the center of one of the walls stretch the carpeting using a "knee kicker." This rental tool allows you to push the goods tight. The tackless strips will grab and hold the carpeting. Repeat the same process until the carpeting is secure all around. Remove temporary tacks as you go.

Trim the carpeting with a carpet trimmer, also a rental item. Push the overlap down between the wall and the strips.

HOW TO APPLY PLASTIC LAMINATE

High-pressure laminate, or simply "laminate," is resin-coated paper that has been laminated under high heat and pressure. The result: a versatile rigid sheet that's excellent for covering kitchen and bathroom countertops, furniture, and cabinets.

A Few Words About Laminate

Laminates are available in an extensive range of patterns and colors; some of them are color-keyed to match kitchen appliances and bathroom fixtures. You may have to special-order the laminate you want, but delivery usually doesn't take long.

Standard laminate sheets are 1/32 and 1/16 inch thick and measure from 2×5 to 5×12 feet. Buy the thin sheets for vertical applications and the thicker ones for horizontal uses.

You can use regular hand and power tools to cut, drill, trim, and form laminate. However, it's not a bad idea to buy an inexpensive notched trowel to use for spreading on the contact cement. This trowel creates a thin, uniform bed of adhesive that ensures good adhesion. An old paintbrush will work, too.

Taking care of laminated surfaces—whether they're in the kitchen, bathroom, or elsewhere—is no chore. Common sense and a modicum of caution will keep plastic laminate looking good for years. Just remember that although laminate is tough, it can be damaged by high heat and some household cleaners that contain abrasives, peroxide, or chlorine.

Step-By-Step How-To

Plastic laminate is one of those materials that become more intriguing the more you work with them. With practice, you can learn to lay it down as well as many pros. Regardless of the project, the techniques remain much the same. So let's discuss a project you may encounter—re-covering a countertop.

First remove the old covering down to the base material. If the base material is badly damaged, tear it out and replace it with plywood. If the surface is in decent shape, sand it smooth or top it with tempered hardboard.

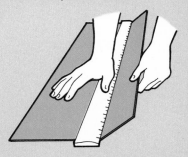

To cut laminate, score its face with a carbide-tipped blade, then hold one side flat, grasp the other, and snap it up.

Or saw the laminate with a fine-tooth back or circular saw. On a table saw, cut with the good face up; with a portable, face-down.

Protect the laminate's edges and corners, because they can chip. And don't bend the material too much; it could snap.

To bond laminate, carefully cut and pre-fit, then apply special

contact cement to the back of the laminate and the bonding surface. Apply all edge pieces first. When the cement is dry to the touch, cover the surface with

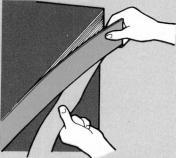

brown wrapping paper, position the laminate, and pull out the sheet. The cement bonds *on contact,* so work carefully. If you do make a mistake, as a last resort fill an oil can with lacquer thinner and squirt it under a corner, peeling the laminate back as you go. Let the thinner dry, and reposition the laminate. You will not need more cement.

When all the laminate is down, roll all surfaces with a rolling pin. Tap along the edges with a hammer and wooden block.

The difference between a professional-looking job and a slapdash job will be in how you trim the edges. You can smooth them by hand with a file, but a router with a laminate bit will save lots of time. File as shown after routing to remove sharp edges.

HOW TO LAY RESILIENT FLOORING

For an average-size room, laying a new vinyl floor is just an afternoon's project. Follow these instructions and beautiful results will be yours.

TILES—Getting Ready

Although new vinyl tiles are versatile enough to be laid over old tiles, wood floors, and concrete, the existing floor must be in good condition and free of oil, wax, and grease. And you must reglue any loose tiles. If you're dealing with a wood floor, you'll need to plane or sand high spots. A concrete floor with a moisture problem requires moisture-proofing and a new subflooring of plywood or particleboard.

Before getting started, read the instructions accompanying your new tile for suggestions. And don't forget to remove the shoe molding before you begin.

Laying Out the Floor

Use a chalk line to strike two intersecting guidelines, each connecting the midpoints on opposite sides of the floor. Temporarily lay one tile at the junction of the chalk lines, fitting one corner squarely at the intersection of the two lines.

Then, form two rows of loose tiles into an "L" that extends to the walls. If the space for the last row of tiles at one or both walls measures less than half the width of a tile, back up the entire "L" half a tile's width and snap new chalk lines.

Installing the Tile

You can purchase resilient vinyl tile with or without adhesive backing. If you choose to apply adhesive, follow the manufacturer's recommendations for the type of adhesive that will work best for you.

With a notched spreader, and working from a corner of the room, lay down enough adhesive to cover one-fourth of the floor (see top sketch). Re-lay the "L"

CHALK LINE

ADHESIVE

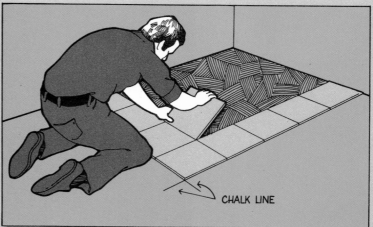

CHALK LINE

GUIDE TILE

TILE BEING MARKED

TILE IN PLACE

permanently; then, fill in the area between with tiles (see middle sketch). Butt each new tile against its neighbor, then *lower* it—don't slide it—into place. Complete the entire floor this way.

If you need to trim tiles for a row that butts against a wall, temporarily position the tile to be trimmed directly over another in the next-to-the-last row (see bottom sketch on previous page). Place a second tile flush against the wall, overlapping the first tile. With the top tile as a guide, score the tile underneath with a sharp knife. The piece you trim off will fit the space you want to fill.

Remove any excess adhesive from the floor with a damp rag. If the adhesive dries, rub it gently with a fine grade of steel wool.

After you complete the entire floor, replace the shoe molding. Give your new floor plenty of time to set before washing or waxing. A week should be sufficient.

SHEET FLOORING— Getting Ready

Prepare your floor surface so that it's free of dirt, grease, wax, and oil. NOTE: Resilient sheet flooring conforms to irregularities of the surface beneath it. For that reason, be sure that the surface you're covering is smooth.

Laying Out the Floor

Resilient sheet flooring most often comes in 12-foot-wide rolls. So if your room is wider than 12 feet, you'll need to plan carefully the location of the seam line. Choose a low-traffic, inconspicuous spot.

When laying out your floor, it's best to do the preliminary work in a large room close to the room in which you'll be laying the new goods. First, roll out the material in the neighboring room so it will reach room temperature. Then remove the shoe molding in the room you're redoing.

Determine which wall is the straightest (this will be the "starting wall" when you roll out the flooring). Choose one edge of the vinyl to correspond to the starting wall and label it.

Next, transfer the measurements of the starting wall to the vinyl. If you have to make a seam, temporarily overlap two

strips so that the patterns match. Draw a line on the bottom sheet (use the edge of the top sheet as a guide) and tape the two together so they don't move while you make other measurements and marks. Add crosshatch marks on both sheets for realignment after you transfer the vinyl.

Add a couple of inches to all the outside dimensions of the sheet(s); you'll cut off the extra during installation. Trim off the excess and cut out any jogs with a sharp linoleum knife or a pair of heavy shears (see top sketch). If necessary, use a contour gauge to transfer intricate cutouts. Make circular cutouts for pipes, radiator legs, or other obstructions.

Installation

After making the needed cuts, roll up the sheet so that the starter edge is on the outside. Carry the roll into the room to be floored. Align the edge with the starter wall and unroll the sheet (see bottom sketch), allowing edges to roll up the wall on all four sides.

For installations requiring a

seam, unroll the goods, using the guidelines you drew to match up the pieces. Then squeeze the overlapping sheets together as tightly as possible (get a helper to stand on the seam) and cut through both pieces of vinyl, using a sharp utility knife and a straightedge. Remove the excess. Fold back both sheets; then spread a strip of seaming cement along the seam line. Butt the edges of the material neatly and press both sheets into the cement.

Finish fitting the vinyl by trimming off the excess edges around the walls, leaving a ⅛-inch space between the floor and the wall. Slit the flooring between the wall edge and any cutouts.

When the vinyl is completely in place and trimmed correctly, turn back the border and spray a special adhesive onto the subfloor (if desired). Press vinyl into the adhesive; replace the shoe molding. When replacing furniture or heavy appliances in a newly floored room, be sure that you use extra care to avoid gouging the material.

WOOD JOINERY TECHNIQUES

No matter what material you're planning to use, it will have to be cut to size—measure twice and cut once is a good rule—then put together using glue, nails or screws, and one of these joints.

Butt Joints

The simplest joint of all, the butt joint, consists of two pieces of wood meeting at a right angle and

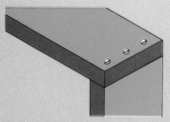

held together with nails, or preferably, screws (see sketch). A dab of glue before using the nails or screws will make the joint even more secure. But don't use glue if you're planning to take the work apart sometime later.

When reinforced by one of the six methods illustrated, the butt joint is effective for making corner

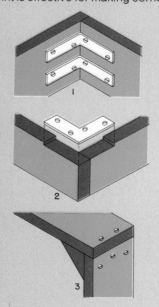

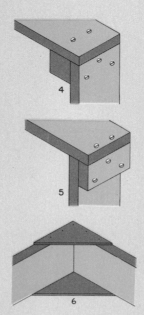

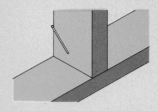

joints. Two common fasteners are metal angles (1), and flat corner plates (2). Using scrap wood, you can reinforce the joint with a triangular wedge (3), or with a square block (4). A variation of the square block places the block on the outside of the joint (5). Finally, a triangular gusset made from plywood or hardboard will also serve to reinforce a corner butt joint (6).

When a butt joint is in the form of a T—for example, in making a framework for light plywood or hardboard—you can reinforce it with a metal angle, T plate, or corrugated fasteners.

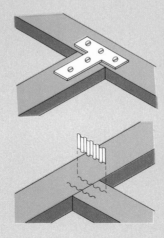

For really rough work, you can drive in a couple of nails at an

angle, or toenail (see sketch). A variation of this is to place a block of wood alongside the crosspiece

and secure it with a couple of nails.

A close cousin to the T joint and the butt joint is the plain overlap joint. It is held in place with at least two screws (see sketch). For extra reinforcement, apply glue between the pieces of wood.

Butt joints are an excellent means of securing backs to various units, especially when appearance is not a factor. Simply cut the back to the outside di-

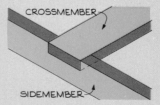

mensions of the work, then nail in place . . . it's called a flush back.

Lap Joints

On those projects where appearance is vital, consider full and half-lap joints. To make a full lap joint, cut a recess in one of the pieces of wood equal in depth to the thickness of the crossmember (see sketch).

The half-lap joint is similar to the full lap joint when finished, but the technique is different. First, cut a recess equal to half the

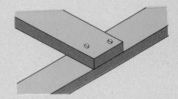

thickness of the crossmember halfway through the crossrail. Then, make a similar cut in the opposite half of the other piece (see sketch on the next page).

Butt joints and overlap joints do

not require any extra work besides cutting the pieces to size. However, full and half-lap joints

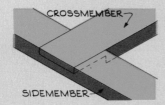

CROSSMEMBER

SIDEMEMBER

require the use of a backsaw and a chisel. For a full-lap joint, mark off the thickness and width of the crossmember on the work in which it is to fit.

Use the backsaw to make a cut at each end that's equal to the thickness of the crossmember, then use a chisel to remove the wood between the backsaw cuts. Check for sufficient depth and finish off with a fine rasp or sandpaper. Apply white glue to the mating surfaces and insert two screws to hold the joint securely.

Dado Joints

The dado joint is a simple way of suspending a shelf from its side supports. To make a dado joint, draw two parallel lines with a knife

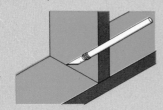

across the face of the work equal to the thickness of the wood it is to engage (see sketch). The depth should be about one-third of the thickness of the wood.

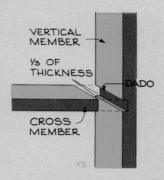

VERTICAL MEMBER

1/3 OF THICKNESS

DADO

CROSS MEMBER

Next, make cuts on these lines and one or more between the lines

with a backsaw. Then, chisel out the wood to the correct depth.

You can speed the job immeasurably by using a router, a bench saw, or a radial arm saw. Any one of these power tools makes the cutting of dadoes an easy job — and provides much greater accuracy than can be achieved by hand.

If appearance is a factor, consider the stopped dado joint. In this type of joint, the dado (the cutaway part) extends only part way, and only a part of the shelf is cut away to match the non-cut part of the dado.

To make a stopped dado, first make your guide marks and chisel away a small area at the stopped end to allow for saw movement. Then make saw cuts

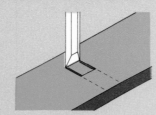

along your guide marks to the proper depth. Next chisel out the waste wood as shown in sketch.

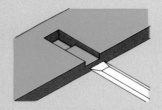

And finally, cut away a corner of the connecting board to accommodate the stopped dado.

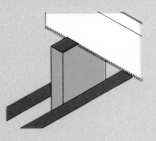

Rabbet Joints

The rabbet joint is really a partial dado. As you can see in the drawing at the top of the following column, only one of the meet-

ing members is cut away.

The rabbet joint is a simple one to construct, and it's quite strong, too. To ensure adequate strength, be sure to secure the meeting members with nails or screws and glue.

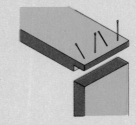

This joint is often used in the construction of inset backs for units such as cabinets and bookshelves (see the sketch below). To make this joint, rabbet each of the framing members, then care-

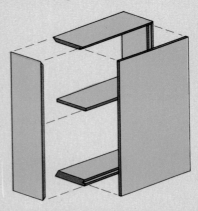

fully measure the distance between the rabbetted openings. Cut the back accordingly. Then use thin screws to secure the back to the unit.

Mortise and Tenon Joints

A particularly strong joint, the mortise and tenon joint is excellent when used for making T joints, right-angle joints, and for joints in the middle of rails. As its name indicates, this joint has two

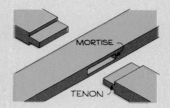

MORTISE

TENON

parts—the *mortise,* which is the open part of the joint, and the *tenon,* the part that fits into the mortise.

Make the mortise first, as it is much easier to fit the tenon to the mortise than the other way around. Divide the rail (the part to be mortised) into thirds and carefully mark off the depth and the width of the opening with a sharp pencil.

Next, use a chisel, equal to the width of the mortise, to remove the wood between the pencil marks. You can expedite this job by drilling a series of holes in the rail with an electric drill, a drill press, or even a hand drill. (If you have a drill press, you can purchase a special mortising bit that will drill square holes, believe it or not.) Mark the drill bit with a bit of tape to indicate the desired depth. Now use the chisel to remove the excess wood.

To make the tenon, divide the rail into thirds, mark the required depth, and use a backsaw to remove unwanted wood. If you have a bench or radial saw, the job of removing the wood will be much easier. Use a dado blade and set the blades high enough to remove the outer third of the wood. Reverse the work and remove the lower third, leaving the inner third intact.

To assemble, make a trial fit, and if all is well, apply some white glue to the tenon and insert it into the mortise. If by chance the tenon is too small for the mortise, simply insert hardwood wedges at top and bottom.

Use moderate clamping pressure on the joint until the glue dries overnight. Too much pressure will squeeze out the glue, actually weakening the joint.

Miter Joints

You can join two pieces of wood meeting at a right angle rather elegantly with a miter joint. And it's not a difficult joint to make. All you need is a miter box and a backsaw, or a power saw that you can adjust to cut at a 45 degree angle.

Since the simple miter joint is a surface joint with no shoulders for support, you must reinforce it. The easiest way to do this is with nails and glue (see sketch at the top of the following column). You'll notice that most picture

frames are made this way.

However, for cabinet and furniture work, you may use other means of reinforcement. One way is to use a hardwood spline as shown in the drawing. Apply glue to the spline and to the mitered

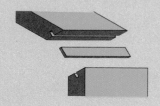

area and clamp as shown until the glue dries.

A variation of the long spline uses several short splines—at least three—inserted at opposing angles.

Dowels are a popular method of reinforcing a mitered joint, too. Careful drilling of the holes is necessary to make certain the dowel holes align. Use dowels that are slightly shorter than the holes they are to enter to allow for glue at the bottom. Score or roughen the

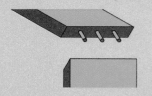

dowels to give the glue a better surface for a strong bond.

Dovetail Joints

The dovetail joint is a sign of good craftsmanship. It's a strong joint especially good for work subject

to heavy loads.

To make the joint, first draw the outline of the pin as shown and

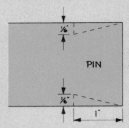

cut away the excess wood with a sharp backsaw. Place the pin over the second piece of wood and draw its outline with a sharp pencil. Make the two side cuts with the backsaw and an additional cut or two to facilitate the next step—chiseling away the excess wood. Then test for fit, apply glue and clamp the pieces until

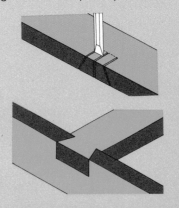

dry. This is the basic way to make most dovetail joints. However, it's much easier to make dovetail joints with a router and dovetail template, especially made for home craftsman use.

Corner Joints

These joints are used for attaching legs to corners for framing. A good technique for joining corners is the three-way joint involving a set of steel braces you can buy. First, insert the bolt into the inside corner of the leg. Then cut slots into the side members, and secure the brace with two screws at each end. Finally, tighten the wing nut.

A variation of the three-way joint uses dowels and a triangular ¾-inch-thick gusset plate for additional reinforcement. To make this joint, first glue the dowels in

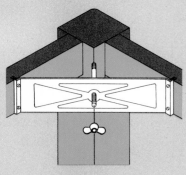

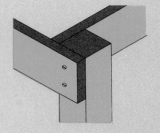

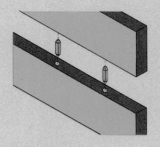

of being fastened to each other, the butted members are each

fastened to the corner post with screws.

Edge-to-Edge Joints

Whenever an extra-wide surface is required, such as a desk top, workbench, or a large storage cabinet, this joint fills the bill. To make it, glue together two or more boards, then hold securely with either bar or pipe clamps. If the boards have a pronounced grain, reverse them side-to-side

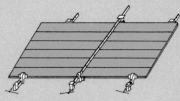

to minimize warping. For additional strength, screw cleats to the underside of the boards.

You also can use hardwood splines to join several boards. Cut a groove the exact width of the spline along the meeting sides of the two boards (see sketch). Cut the grooves slightly deeper than the spline width and in the exact center of the board thickness. The best way to cut such grooves is with a router or a table saw.

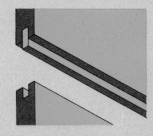

Then assemble with glue and clamps.

Another possibility for joining several boards involves the use of dowels. To make this joint, first

make holes in the boards. You can either use a doweling jig or a drill. If you use a drill, first drive

brads (small finishing nails) into one board and press them against the second board to leave marks for drilling. Make the dowel holes slightly deeper than the dowels. Score the dowels, apply glue, join the two boards together, and clamp with pipe or bar clamps until the glue sets (allow plenty of time).

If you'll be drilling many dowel holes, you may want to use a wood or metal template to ensure accurate spacing.

Box Joints

One joint is so common in the construction of boxes — and drawers — it's called a *box joint,* or a *finger joint because its parts* look like the outstretched fingers of a hand (see sketch). Note that one of the mating pieces must have two end fingers, or one more

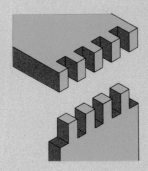

finger than the piece it is to engage. You can make this joint by hand with a backsaw and a small, sharp chisel. However, it is much easier, quicker, and more accurate to make it on a table saw. Use a dado blade set to the desired width and proper depth of the fingers and mark off the waste area so there will be no mistake as to what you want to cut away.

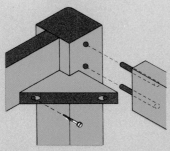

the vertical piece (see sketch). Let them dry completely, then finish the assembly.

A glued miter joint, reinforced with screws and glue, also makes a good corner joint. Make sure the screws do not penetrate the outside surface of the mitered joint.

Probably the strongest of the corner joints is the mortise and tenon (with mitered ends) reinforced with screws (see sketch). The miters on the ends of the tenons allow for a buildup of glue in the mortise, which in turn makes the joint stronger. Make sure that the holes you drill for the screws are not in line with each other.

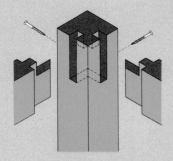

Otherwise, the wood may split. Use flathead screws and countersink the holes.

The simplest corner joint of all is a butt joint for the two horizontal members (see sketch). Instead

SUPPORT SYSTEMS

Any item you construct, no matter how light, must be capable of supporting itself as well as its "payload". Even a simple box has a support system: its sides are self-supporting, each one serving to support and strengthen its neighbor.

How to Attach Things to Walls

Many items, such as shelves and wall-hung cabinets, depend on the wall as part of their support system. However, you can't always drive a nail or insert a screw just anywhere in a wall. For best stability, drive them into the studs of the wall.

Locating studs. One way of locating wall studs is to rap the wall with your knuckles. Listen for a "solid" sound. (Thumps between the studs will sound hollow.) This works fine if you have excellent hearing.

A far easier way is to buy an inexpensive stud finder. Its magnetic needle will respond to hidden nails, indicating the presence of a stud.

Locating one stud does not necessarily mean that the next stud is 16 inches away, though. It should be, but many times it isn't. For example, if the framework of a door or wall falls 20 inches away from the last stud, the builder may have left a 20-inch gap between them. Or, a stud may have been placed midway, leaving 10-inch spaces on either side.

Fastening to hollow-core walls. Quite often, because of physical requirements, you will need to make an installation between studs into a hollow plaster wall.

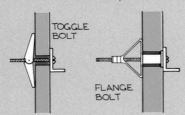

What then? The answer is to use flange or toggle bolts. They distribute their load over a wide area,

and if used in sufficient number and with discretion, they'll hold a fairly heavy load.

Fastening to masonry. Attaching items to a masonry wall is not difficult. if you're working with a brick, concrete, or cinder block wall, use a carbide-tipped drill to make a hole *in the mortar*. Make the hole deep and wide enough to accept a wall plug. Then insert the screw or bolt to fasten the item in place (see sketch).

Another method of fastening to

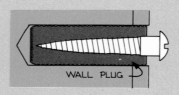

WALL PLUG

masonry walls is to drill a ½-inch hole in the *mortar* and pound a hardwood dowel into the hole. Bevel the end of the dowel and lightly coat it with grease before driving it in place. Then drill a pilot hole in the middle of the dowel and continue with the fastening.

If by chance you must drill into the brick part of a wall rather than the mortar, don't despair. Again use a carbide-tipped drill, but this time start with a ¼-inch bit, and finish with the larger size desired.

How to Mount Units On a Base

If your project is any type of cabinet, a base is a good idea. A base should provide toe space of at least 3½ inches in height and 2¾ inches in depth. If you plan to mount the unit on casters, you'll automatically get toe space that makes the project convenient.

Box base. This easy-to-build recessed base consists of a four-sided open box installed at the

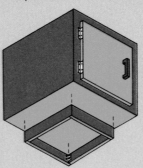

bottom of the cabinet or storage unit. Since appearance is not a factor, you can construct the box with simple butt joints and secure it to the cabinet with steel angle brackets installed along the inside of the base (see sketch).

Leg base. Four short, stubby legs also make a good base. Commercial legs come with their own mounting plate, which is screwed to the bottom of the cabinet before the leg is screwed into place (see sketch). You can also install home-built legs with hanger bolts.

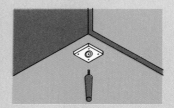

These bolts have a "wood" thread on one end and a coarse "machine" thread on the other end. Drill an undersize hole in the cabinet for the machine end, insert the hanger bolt using pliers and screw the leg into place.

A good source for low-priced legs is a lumberyard that does millwork. Quite often, they'll have a bin full of legs of all sizes that may have slight imperfections or chips which won't affect their serviceability.

How to Mount Shelves

Shelves are a quick and easy way of getting additional storage space in your home, shop, or garage. The best material for shelving is ¾-inch plywood or pine boards—8, 10, 12 inches wide, depending on the items to be stored. To prevent sagging, install a shelf support every 30 inches. And don't use hardboard or chip board, as they tend to bow under heavy loads.

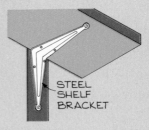

STEEL SHELF BRACKET

Shelf brackets. The easiest way to mount a shelf is by means of steel shelf brackets sold in hardware stores (see sketch). Ask for brackets whose short leg is nearly equal to the *width* of the shelf you plan to install. And always mount the brackets with the *long* leg against the wall. Screw the brackets into the wall and space them about 30 inches apart. For heavy loads, shop around for brackets that have gussets connecting the two legs. Brackets without gussets tend to sway under heavy loads.

Cleats and angle brackets. The narrow space between two walls is an ideal location for shelving. Simply install a pair of cleats at the heights where you want shelves (see sketch). Use cleats that are at least ¾ inch thick and as long as the shelf is wide.

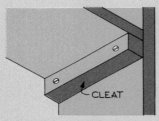

CLEAT

If the walls are of masonry, secure the cleats with so-called steel cut nails (wear goggles when driving these, as they may break off if not struck head-on). Secure the cleats with screws if the walls are of wood, or use flange bolts if they're hollow.

You can also use small steel angle brackets. Mount two under each side of the shelf as shown.

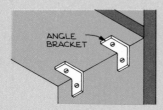

ANGLE BRACKET

Dowels. Another method of supporting shelves is with dowels. Drill holes equal to the diameter of the dowels, and bore them deep enough to accept at least ½-inch of dowel length. (Make sure both left and right holes are the same height; you might use a level on the shelves to ensure exact mounting.)

Use ¼-inch dowels for light-duty shelves and ⅜-inch dowels for shelves supporting heavy loads. Beveling the dowel ends

will make them easier to insert into the holes. To change shelf spacing, simply drill additional holes.

Dado cuts. This method of supporting shelves has long been a favorite with master cabinetmakers. First, determine the height of the shelf, mark the uprights, and make your cuts. Then cut the shelf to fit.

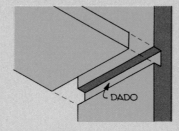

DADO

Metal tracks and brackets. You can recess or surface-mount these handy shelf supports. Shelf brackets, specially designed to fit into the track slots, are made to accept 8-, 10-, and 12-inch-wide shelves. Special brackets which adjust to hold shelves at a downward slope also are available and are used to hold dictionaries and reference books.

These tracks and brackets are available in finishes to match the decor of practically any room.

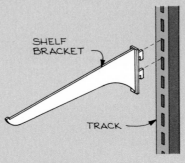

SHELF BRACKET

TRACK

When installing shelves in a cabinet, mount two tracks on each side of the cabinet and use small clips to hold the shelves in place. To change the spacing between shelves, just remove the clips and reposition.

Furring strips. These are especially useful for supporting and erecting shelves in the garage or workshop. Use 2x4s bolted or screwed to the wall and short lengths of 1x4s for shelf supports, as indicated in the drawing. Note that one end is dadoed into the 2x4 (½-inch depth is enough). The

front end of the shelf support bracket is supported by a 1x4 cut at a 45 degree angle at the bottom and engages a cutout called a *bird's mouth* at the top. Toenail

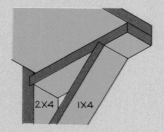

2X4   1X4

the lower end of the 1x4 into the 2x4. There's no need to nail the upper end, as the weight of the shelf will keep it in place.

Support from above. While most shelves are supported from the bottom, you can also support them from the top. This top support method is especially applicable in basement areas where the joists are exposed. You can nail 2x4s to the joists and fit any type of

project—open shelves, a cabinet, even a work surface between them. If the project to be suspended will run perpendicular to the joists, be careful to plan the length so that it will match the spacing of the joists.

Another way to support shelving from the top is use threaded rods (see sketch above). Choose rods from ¼- to ¾-inch diameter according to the load you'll support. Drill holes in the shelves slightly oversize. To attach the upper end of the rod, drill holes in 2x2 scraps and screw to the joists. Insert the rod and add a nut and washer to the top.

Then install the shelves with a nut and washer on both top and bottom. Tighten the nuts securely to give the shelves as much stability as possible.

HOW TO MAKE DRAWERS

Next to shelves, drawers are the most convenient place for storage. And a drawer is comparatively easy to build. It's just a five-sided box, connected at its corners with the joints previously described.

Types of Drawers

Drawers, no matter how they're made, fall into two general classifications—the flush or recessed type, and the lip type.

Flush drawers. You must fit this type of drawer carefully to the cabinet opening, with only enough clearance at top and sides to facilitate sliding in and out. In fact, some custom cabinetmakers often will make flush-type drawers with a taper of 1/16 inch from front to back to ensure a good appearance and an easy-sliding fit.

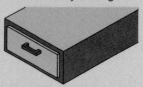

Lipped drawers. These drawers have an oversize front panel that completely covers the drawer opening and so offers much greater leeway in fitting the drawer into its recess.

One way to make a lipped drawer is to rabbet the front panel to the sides and bottom of the drawer, leaving an overlap of ½ inch or so. A simpler way is to screw a false front to the finished drawer front. With this method, if there is any error in construction, the false front will hide it. Attach the drawer front with countersunk flathead screws from the *inside* of the drawer. In addition to the screws, apply white glue between the two pieces.

Construction Details

When making drawers, remember to make the cabinet first, then fit the drawers to the cabinet openings. To make a drawer, first determine its length and cut two pieces of wood to this size and the required width. (The width, of course, will be the height of the finished drawer.)

Draw two parallel lines, equal to the thickness of the drawer back, about ½ inch from the ends

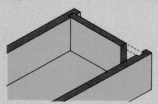

of the two pieces. Cut a dado between these lines to a depth of ¼ inch.

Next, measure the inside distance between the two sides of the drawer opening and cut the drawer back to this measurement. (Allow for clearance and the depth of the dado cuts in the drawer sides.)

For the front of the drawer, plan simple butt joints and cut it to allow a ¼-inch overhang on all sides, if you plan a lip.

You are now ready to partially assemble the drawer. Brush some white glue into the two dado cuts and install the back panel. Use three or four brads at each joint to secure the sides. Next attach the drawer front using glue and brads or screws to secure it to the sides.

A false front nailed or screwed to the existing front from the inside of the drawer will conceal the original brads or screws. If you use brads, countersink them with a nail set.

The bottom of the drawer consists of ¼-inch or thicker plywood, and is nailed to the sides and back of the drawer. For stronger, more elaborate construction, you can use any one of the woodworking joints described earlier in this section.

Drawer Runners and Guides

To ensure that the drawers you build will move in and out without wobbling, you can use any one of

three methods: guides located at each side of the drawer; a central guide placed at the bottom of the drawer; or commercial metal tracks mounted on the sides of the cabinet with nylon wheels on the drawer sides. These come in lengths to fit most drawers and are especially good for heavy loads. Select them before you build the drawer in order to plan the clearance space.

The simplest guide consists of two narrow lengths of wood secured to each side of the drawer, spaced an inch apart (see sketch). Another strip of wood, mounted on each side of the

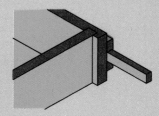

drawer opening, fits the "track" mounted on the drawer sides. To ease operation, apply paste wax to all touching surfaces.

For guides at the bottom of the drawer, mount lengths of wood on the cabinet and engage the two strips of wood on the bottom of the drawer.

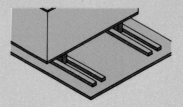

If you're planning to incorporate runners and guides in the drawers, make allowances before starting work. A clearance of ½-inch is required for guides mounted at the sides of the drawers, and 1 inch for center-mounted guides. Regardless of what type of drawer guides you use, make sure you install them accurately.

You can even make easy-sliding drawers without guides or runners by installing plastic glides in the drawer openings so the bottom of the drawer will bear against plastic instead of wood. Steel thumbtacks also ease drawer movement. But don't forget to apply wax to the bottom bearing surfaces of the drawer.

HOW TO INSTALL CABINET DOORS

Except for shelves, tables, and chairs, nearly every piece of furniture you build will have some sort of door. All doors require hinges or tracks, and handles for opening and closing. Here are the basics.

Construction Pointers

To prevent warping, cabinet doors should be at least ½ inch thick. However, you can use a ¼-inch panel, providing you frame it with ½-inch wood, somewhat like a picture frame.

If you plan to laminate a door panel with plastic, use the thin grade laminate especially made for vertical surfaces. The heavy grade, made for countertops, may cause the cabinet to warp.

Sliding Doors

Sliding doors are easier to fit and install than swinging doors, and, as a rule, are of much lighter stock than conventional doors. Track for sliding doors can be aluminum or plastic (left sketch), or it can consist of grooves cut into the top and bottom of the framework (right sketch).

Of course, you must cut these grooves before assembly. Make the upper grooves about twice as deep as the bottom ones so you can lift up, then lower the door into place. The doors should be flush with the bottom shelf surface when it's touching the top of the upper groove.

To ease sliding, apply wax or a silicone spray to the grooves. If you're planning to use handles, recess them into the door so there will be no interference when the doors bypass each other.

Hinged Doors

Flush-type hinged doors that recess within the framing require clearance all around to prevent binding. To install a flush-type door, make a dry fit, and if the door fits, insert small wedges at all sides to hold it in place and ensure clearance until the hinges have been completely installed.

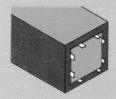

Then place the hinge against the door—if it's an exterior mounting—and mark the hinge holes with an awl. Drill pilot holes and install the hinges. Use this same procedure if you have an interior mounting job.

With hinges that are partly concealed—half on the inside of the door and half on the frame—mount the hinges on the door first, set the door in place, and mark the location of the hinge on the frame or door jamb. This method is much easier than trying to fit an already-mounted hinge to the blind or interior part of the door.

Types of hinges. There are literally dozens of types of hinges to choose from. Following are a few of the more common varieties.

As a general rule, you should mortise hinges into cabinets so they are flush with the work. However, always surface mount decorative hinges, such as colonial, rustic, and ornamental hinges.

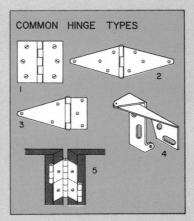

COMMON HINGE TYPES

(1) *Butt hinges* are the type you're probably most familiar with. Use them for either right- or left-hand doors. The larger sizes have re-

movable pins to facilitate taking off the door; the smaller sizes don't. For long cabinet doors or lids. use a piano hinge (a long butt hinge) rather than several smaller ones. (2, 3) The *strap hinge* and the *T hinge* are used for extra-heavy doors. There's no need to mortise these hinges, as they are strictly functional.

(4) *Pivot hinges,* also called knife hinges, are available in different shapes and are especially good for use on ¾-inch plywood doors. All shapes present a very unobtrusive appearance.

(5) *Double-acting hinges* allow a door to be swung from either direction.

Self-closing hinges operate by means of a spring concealed within the barrel of the hinge. Another type, used on kitchen cabinets, has no spring, yet closes the door with a positive snapping action. Its secret is a square shoulder next to the pin.

Special-purpose hinges are available with offset leaves (so the door will overlap the framing); hinges with knuckles (for quick door removal); ball-bearing hinges lubricated for life (for extra-heavy doors); hinges that will automatically raise a door when it is opened (so that it will clear a carpet on the far side of the door); burglar-resistant hinges (with pins that can't be removed when they're on the outside); and hinges that allow a door to be swung back far enough so that the full width of the doorway can be utilized.

Door catches and handles. In addition to hinges, you will need hardware to keep the doors closed and to lock them. For cabinet work, your best hardware bets are spring-loaded or magnetic catches.

Spring-loaded catches come with single and double rollers and are ideal for lipped doors, flush doors, double doors, and shelves. These catches are adjustable.

Install magnetic catches so there is physical contact between the magnet in the frame and the "keeper" on the door.

A handle of some type is required for all drawers and doors. Handles can be surface-mounted or recessed flush with the drawer or door. Sliding doors always use recessed handles so the doors can bypass each other.

THE HARDWARE YOU'LL NEED

For any sort of fastening work, you will need nails, screws, and bolts, as well as glues and cements.

Nails, Screws, and Bolts

These most common of all fastening materials are available in diverse widths and lengths, and in steel, brass, aluminum, copper, and even stainless steel.

Nails. Nails are sold by the penny—which has nothing to do with their cost. The "penny," (abbreviated *d*) refers to the size. The chart shows a box nail marked in the penny size designations as well as actual lengths in inches.

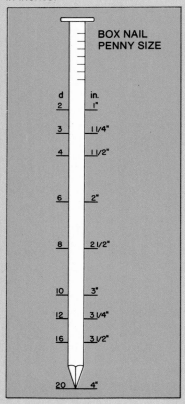

BOX NAIL PENNY SIZE

d	in.
2	1"
3	1 1/4"
4	1 1/2"
6	2"
8	2 1/2"
10	3"
12	3 1/4"
16	3 1/2"
20	4"

Use common and box nails for general-purpose work; finish and casing nails for trim or cabinetwork; and brads for attaching molding to walls and furniture.

COMMON SCREWS

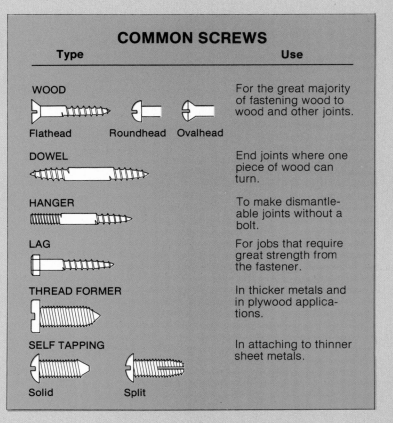

Type	Use
WOOD — Flathead, Roundhead, Ovalhead	For the great majority of fastening wood to wood and other joints.
DOWEL	End joints where one piece of wood can turn.
HANGER	To make dismantleable joints without a bolt.
LAG	For jobs that require great strength from the fastener.
THREAD FORMER	In thicker metals and in plywood applications.
SELF TAPPING — Solid, Split	In attaching to thinner sheet metals.

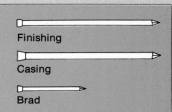

Finishing

Casing

Brad

Screws. Screws are sold by length and diameter. The diameter is indicated by a number, from 1 to 16. The thicker the screw shank, the larger the number. The drawing shows some of the most popular types of screws.

Always drill a pilot hole when inserting a screw into hardwood. And always drill a clearance hole in the leading piece of wood when screwing two pieces of wood together. Without a clearance hole, the leading piece tends to "hang up," preventing a tight fit between the two.

Bolts. You can also fasten wood together with bolts, but only if there is access to the back for the required washer and nut. A bolted joint is stronger than a screwed joint, as the bolt diameter is generally thicker than the comparable screw, and also because the wrench used to tighten the nut can apply much more force than a screwdriver in a screw slot.

Glues and Cements

While not "hardware" as such, glue is an important adjunct to any fastening job. The so-called white glue is excellent for use with wood, and only moderate clamping pressure is required. When dry, it is crystal clear. However, it's not waterproof so don't use it for work subject to excessive dampness—and of course, never for outdoor use. Use the two-tube epoxy "glue" for joints that must be waterproof.

Plastic resin glue, a powder that you mix with water to a creamy consistency, is highly water resistant.

Contact cement provides an excellent bond between wood and wood, and wood and plastic. When working with contact cement, remember that it dries instantly, so position your surfaces

COMMON BOLTS

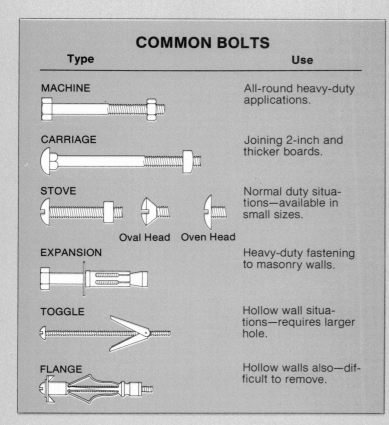

Type	Use
MACHINE	All-round heavy-duty applications.
CARRIAGE	Joining 2-inch and thicker boards.
STOVE (Oval Head / Oven Head)	Normal duty situations—available in small sizes.
EXPANSION	Heavy-duty fastening to masonry walls.
TOGGLE	Hollow wall situations—requires larger hole.
FLANGE	Hollow walls also—difficult to remove.

The plate type caster is merely screwed to the bottom by four screws that pass through holes in the plate. They are not height adjustable unless, of course, you use shims.

All casters use ball bearings as part of the plate assembly to facilitate swiveling. For extra-heavy usages, purchase casters with ball-bearing wheels as well.

The wheels on casters are of two types—plastic or rubber. Use casters with plastic wheels if the project is to be rolled on a soft surface such as a rug; rubber wheeled casters are best on hard concrete, vinyl, or hardwood. It's a good idea to use graphite to lubricate the wheels and their bearings, as oil tends to pick up dust and dirt.

To prevent a caster-equipped unit from rolling, get locking casters. A small lever on the outside of the wheel locks a "brake." Brakes on only two of the four casters on a unit are sufficient.

Miscellaneous Hardware

There are many types of hardware that can come in handy when you're constructing storage bins, cabinets, chests, shelves, and other projects.

Following are some you may need from time to time: corrugated fasteners connect two boards or mend splits in wood; metal angles reinforce corners; flat and T plates also reinforce work; masonry nails secure work to concrete or brick walls; steel plates with a threaded center are used for attaching legs to cabinets; screw eyes and cup hooks allow for hanging items inside storage units; and lag screw plugs made of lead or plastic secure furring strips or shelf brackets to masonry walls.

You'll be wise to stock your workshop with most of these items in a couple of sizes. That way, you won't have to make a special trip when they're needed.

When to Use What Glue

Type	Use
White glue (No mixing)	Paper, cloth, wood
Epoxy (requires mixing)	Wood, metal, stone (waterproof)
Plastic resin (requires mixing)	Wood to wood (water resistant)
Contact cement (no mixing)	Wood to wood or plastic (waterproof)
Waterproof glue (requires mixing)	Wood to wood (waterproof)

together exactly as you want them. You won't get a second chance.

True waterproof glue comes in two containers; one holds a liquid resin, the other a powder catalyst. When dry, this glue is absolutely waterproof and can be safely used for garden equipment and all outdoor projects and furniture.

Glides and Casters

The intended use determines whether a piece of furniture needs a caster or a glide. If you don't plan to move it frequently, use a glide; otherwise, a caster is the best choice.

Glides come in many sizes, determined by the glide area touching the floor, and with steel or plastic bottoms. The simple nail-on glides aren't height adjustable but you can adjust screw glides by screwing the glide in or out to prevent wobbling if the floor is uneven, or if by some chance, the project does not have an even base.

Casters are made in two styles—stem type (only the stem type is adjustable) and plate type (at left in sketch). The stem type requires a hole to be drilled into the leg or base of the cabinet or furniture. This hole accepts a sleeve that in turn accepts the stem of the caster.

FINISHING TECHNIQUES

Finishing is your final job before you can step back and admire your work. Before starting, make sure that all nails are flush or countersunk and filled, all flathead screws are flush with the surface, all cracks are filled, and all surfaces are sanded and cleaned.

Hardboard and Chip Board

If the unit you have built is made of hardboard, about the only finish you can apply to it is paint. No preparation is needed except to remove any oil or dirt. Inasmuch as hardboard is brown—the tempered type is a darker brown—you'll need to apply at least two coats of paint if you want the final finish to be a light color.

Hardboard will accept latex or alkyd paints equally well. Between coats, let dry overnight and then sand lightly.

You also can paint chip board, flake board, and particle board, but because of their slightly rougher texture you should apply a "filler" coat of shellac first, then proceed with painting.

Plywood

Because of its comparatively low cost, fir plywood is used extensively for building projects. However, the hard and soft growth patterns in the wood will show through unless a sealer is used before painting or finishing with varnish or lacquer.

After sealing, sand lightly and finish with at least two coats of paint, varnish, or lacquer. The final step for varnish or lacquer work consists of an application of paste wax applied with fine steel wool and polishing with terry cloth or any other coarse-textured cloth.

Plywood has a pronounced end grain due to its layered construction. If your project will be on display, it's best to hide the end grain, and there are several ways to do this.

A mitered joint is the obvious solution, as then the end grain is hidden within the joint. Another solution is wood veneer tape (see sketch). This tape comes in rolls and is really walnut, oak, mahogany, or a similar wood in a very thin strip about ¾ inch wide. Either glue it or use contact cement, applying the cement to the tape and to the plywood edges. When the cement has lost its gloss, carefully align the tape and press over the plywood edge.

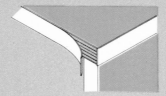

You also can use molding to cover the edges. It has the additional advantage of making a decorative edge requiring no further treatment.

Metal molding is another option, especially useful for edges which are subject to wear and abuse.

A rabbet joint will also hide end grain. Make the rabbet deep enough so that only the last ply is uncut.

Other Woods

If your project is constructed of a fine wood, a more elaborate finishing technique is needed.

Sanding. You can do this by hand or with a power sander. A power belt sander is fine for initial sanding, but always do the final sanding with an orbital or straight line finishing sander—or with fine sandpaper.

Filling and staining. Open grain woods such as oak, chestnut, walnut, ash, and mahogany require a filler to close their pores. Apply the filler with a brush or rag, wiping across the grain. After 10 or 15 minutes, remove the excess filler with a coarse cloth.

If a stain is called for, let the wood dry for 24 hours before application. A stain applied over a filler that has not dried will show up as a "hot" spot.

Sealing. A sealer, as its name implies, is used to seal the stains and filler from the subsequent finishing coats.

One of the best sealers is shellac. One advantage of using shellac is that it prevents the stain from bleeding. Thin the shellac with alcohol to the consistency of light cream; as it comes in the can, it's much too thick for use as a sealer. You can also use ready-mixed stains combined with a sealer.

Finishes. *Varnish,* the traditional finish for wood, is available in many types and colors.

To prepare a piece for varnish, sand it lightly, wipe off the dust with a turpentine-dampened rag, and apply the varnish with long, flowing strokes. Do not brush out the varnish as you would paint. And don't use varnish during humid weather. To make sure the varnish will flow evenly, place the can in warm water.

Varnish requires at least two coats, with a minimum of 24 hours drying time. Sand lightly between coats. After the second or third coat has dried for at least a week, rub down with steel wool and paste wax. Polish with a rough cloth.

Shellac, too, will yield super results. It's fairly easy to work with and it dries dust free in a half-hour. You can apply the second coat within two hours. Sanding is not required between coats, as the second coat tends to partially dissolve and melt into the first one.

One disadvantage of shellac is that it shows a ring if a liquor-stained glass is placed on a shellac-finished surface. Also, shellac sometimes tends to crack if exposed to dampness.

Polyurethane is a tough synthetic varnish that resists abrasion, alcohol, and fruit stains. It's great for floors, furniture, walls, and woodwork. To apply polyurethane the surface must be clean, dry, and free of grease, oil, and wax. Don't apply a polyurethane finish over previously shellacked or lacquered surfaces. Allow at least 12 hours drying time for each coat, and clean your brushes with mineral spirits or turpentine.

Lacquer is a fast-drying finish you can apply by spray or brush. For spraying, thin lacquer only with lacquer thinner. *Never use turpentine or mineral spirits.*

To brush lacquer, always use a brush that has *never* been used to apply paint.

And never apply lacquer over a painted surface, as the lacquer will lift the paint. As with shellac, sanding between coats is not necessary.